solving the social media puzzle

solving the social media puzzle

7 simple steps to planning a social media marketing strategy for your business

Kathryn Rose
Apryl Parcher

TATE PUBLISHING
AND ENTERPRISES, LLC

Solving the Social Media Puzzle

Published by Tate Publishing & Enterprises, LLC
127 E. Trade Center Terrace | Mustang, Oklahoma 73064 USA
1.888.361.9473 | www.tatepublishing.com

Tate Publishing is committed to excellence in the publishing industry. The company reflects the philosophy established by the founders, based on Psalm 68:11,
"The Lord gave the word and great was the company of those who published it."

Cover Design by Erika Ruggiero

Published in the United States of America

ISBN: 978-1-62147-767-9
Business & Economics / Strategic Planning
12.07.06

Acknowledgements

Many hours of labor and love went into creating this book, and we would like to thank everyone who had a hand in helping us get there:

To our husbands, whose unfailing support and insight got us through the sleepless nights and wee-hour edits—we're very lucky to have you, and so glad you still love us!

To our children, from grownups to newborns, who patiently waited for snippets of Mom's time and rewarded us with hugs and kisses when we needed them most—we love you, too!

To our network of social media consultants—a million thanks! Over the years we've developed many social media alliances and mastermind groups. In fact, the power of social networking has expanded our horizons well beyond anything we could have imagined just five short years ago. Across the country and across the globe, those connections have helped us grow our businesses, and have made us some very dear friends. We're grateful for those continued friendships.

To the expert contributors and business owners who added so much value to the pages of this book, we offer our eternal gratitude. It's one thing to call yourself an expert, but quite another to prove it. Your stories and insights have added immeasurably to this effort, and we truly appreciate your willingness to share your time and expertise.

To Mari Smith and Mike Stelzner, business mentors who came along at just the right time in our lives and helped us reach for new horizons… thank you for your continued inspiration and support.

Table of Contents

Introduction

This is an interesting time in our history. We find ourselves riding the crest of a technological wave that seemed to scoop us up from behind and fling us headlong into an uncertain future. Some of us were blindsided by it (and are still coughing and spluttering), some saw it coming and started swimming early, and the younger set ran out to meet the wave, surfboards under their arms, ready to take on the adventure.

Change, as they say, is inevitable. But it's also happening faster to us than it did to our parents and grandparents. The advent of the Internet, social media and mobile technologies has forever changed how we communicate and how we do business—but many of us are still struggling with these new technologies. Plus, the social evolution is still happening, shifting the landscape under our feet. It's like trying to piece together one of those giant puzzles, but the pieces keep changing after you think you've got it worked out.

Are you having trouble with that puzzle? Do the pieces look different every time you sit down to work on it? If so, then this book is for you. Between these pages, we've mapped out a 7-step plan for taking a high-level view of the social media landscape, selecting the pieces that fit your particular business niche, and working them into your overall marketing strategy without getting lost or distracted along the way.

We've designed this book to be a quick read, and have included some simple exercises you can work on to help you keep your "eye on the prize." We've also included interviews with some of the top minds in the social space; marketers who have a firm grasp of how to incorporate this fast-changing medium into your business.

We hope the information in these pages will help you come away with a clearer idea of where to start with social media. It will serve as a simple guide for selecting the right pieces (and throwing away what doesn't fit) and we also provide a number of links and tools in the book which you will find listed in the Resources section beginning on page 135.

We have also designed a companion workbook to complement this planning guide, which you can find at

http://solvingthesocialmediapuzzle.com/workbook.

Are you ready to jump in? Great! Let's clear the table and get started.

Planning for Success

Why Plan?

Who wants to sit down and plan? No one, really. And we have to admit, when we got started in social media marketing, the idea of planning nearly made us break out in hives. Everyone knows that planning is the key to business success, but most of us still don't take the time to do it.

As we began to get deeper into the social space, however, we discovered that the ONLY way to be successful and not have our time eaten up by last minute things was to have a plan. If social media was going to drive results for us and our clients, we needed to have a roadmap to get us there.

The social phenomenon is evolving as we speak, with new platforms and technologies opening up every day. There is a lot of pressure out there to jump in feet first to stay ahead of the competition, but as many companies have found out the hard way, leaping at every new platform that comes out just to be "first" in the space is often counterproductive. With limited time and resources, you have to pick your battles—and the only way to do that effectively is to write out your goals and objectives, and plot a good map for getting there.

Because social media is fed by content, you need to have a content strategy in place before you start posting. How will you create the content you share? Will it be housed on your website or blog? How often will you update this content?

We spend a fair amount of time in the planning phase for our clients, and it saves a lot of trouble later on. But don't worry—it's not hard—and once you get the hang of it, your roadmap will always be clear.

Our tools are simple. We use blogging and content calendars that help us keep track of the different themes and ideas we will use to create content for ourselves and our clients. As our gift to you, we have designed a calendar for you to download free from our website, www.*solvingthesocialmediapuzzle.com/calendar.*

Our formulas are simple as well. If you remember nothing else about this book, remember this acronym: PETT. It stands for plan, execute, track and tweak. These are the cornerstones of a successful social media strategy. In this book we will give you examples of how to formulate a successful plan, how to execute that plan, what you can do to track your results and what it means to tweak your strategy (you always need to tweak, both when things are working and when they're not).

Social media platforms may be changing on a daily basis, but if you have a plan in place, you will be less likely to panic when Facebook changes its design or Twitter adds a new feature. It won't matter to you, except that perhaps you may have to add a couple of things to your plan or take some things out. Your community building and loyal fan base will follow you no matter what Facebook or Twitter does, as long as you keep that little acronym in mind and plan, execute, track and tweak.

We would also like you to use this guide, plan your strategy and commit to it for the next 60 days. If you define your target markets, set your goals and pick one or two social networks to commit to learning and using over that time period, perhaps social media marketing won't be as overwhelming as you think.

Below are some statistics from *thesocialskinny.com* on business use of social media for 2012[1] to give you an idea of how social has changed our behaviors in the last few years.

Social Media for Business Statistics 2012

- 36% of social media users post brand-related content
- Two out of three social media users believe Twitter influences purchases
- 50% of people follow brands in social media
- 75% of companies now use Twitter as a marketing channel
- 60% of employees would like help from employers to share relevant content
- 40% of companies admit to having no training or governance of social media
- 41% of the class of 2011 used social media in their job search
- 38% of CEOs label social media a high priority, and 57% of businesses plan to hike their social media spend in 2012
- One in three small businesses are now using social media
- 89% of agencies said they would use Facebook to advertise for their clients in 2012, either by purchasing ads, creating pages, or other methods of engagement
- 39% of agencies said they would focus on Twitter, 36% YouTube, 21% LinkedIn and 18% Google+
- Posts from Facebook pages with 10,000 fans reach 30 to 40% of their fans, posts from pages with 100,000 fans reach 20 to 30% of their fans, and posts from pages with 1,000,000 or more fans reach 10% of their fans

As you can see, social media has shifted the way we think about marketing our businesses. Like it or not, it's a permanent change in the way we talk to each other online. However, as with any marketing initiative, it's important to start with the "people" side of things first. So let's get started with the most critical step in making social media work for your business—getting to know your ideal customer.

Who is Your Ideal Customer?

Social media marketing is a bit different from the traditional marketing you're probably used to. While every good marketing plan foundation is built on the target market, it is extremely important in social media to be customer-centric instead of advertising focused. Think about letting your customers come to you through the relationships you build with them. One of the great things about social media marketing is that it allows you to create and sustain long term relationships with your constituency. You can speak directly to them through tweets, posts and videos.

So how are you going to find your ideal customer and build a long term relationship? One easy way to start is to think about your product in terms of who it serves. Then ask yourself, "What problems can I solve for people that will make them want to do business with me or my company?"

In traditional marketing plans, target markets are sometimes defined very broadly, such as "women, aged 25-54, with $100k+ income." That's much too wide a spectrum for social media where you are interacting with real people who want to have authentic, real conversations. You need to define them more specifically.

One of the best exercises to use when defining your target market is to create "personas." Essentially, you give your target market an actual name, face and characteristics of a real person. This approach goes beyond traditional demographics and can help you reach and communicate with your target audience faster.

A good way to start is by using your current clients. Make a list of your top clients. What do they have in common? Break it down into the basics: What are their needs? Why do they buy your products? What movies do they like? What TV shows do they watch? Do they have children? What hobbies do they enjoy? The more detailed you can get, the better. If you are having a difficult time with this exercise, consider sending out a survey to your customer base. There are free survey tools available such as *Survey Monkey* you can use for very simple client surveys (all tools referenced will be at the back of the book under the "resources" section). This may help you in your target market building. If you want faster results, pick up the phone! People will be thrilled you asked for their opinion, they may even tell you things about your business they might not have otherwise.

Creating personas can be particularly effective when you are marketing solely online. For example, when Kathryn wrote *The Parent's Guide to Facebook*,, she had a limited marketing budget so she decided to use an online influencer strategy. She identified the influencers in the Mom Blog space and reached out to them to ask them to review the book. She used Google to look up the Top 50 Mom Blogs and read them all, then broke her target market into three main personas:

1. **Social Sally the Soccer Mom:** Sally loves to be involved with her kids and thinks it's funny that they post silly pictures of themselves partying and acting crazy. She doesn't realize this is going to be part of her children's digital footprint and can affect them later in life.

2. **Pumpkin Sweater Peggy:** Peggy is the type of woman who used to dress trendy and hip, but once she had a child everything changed. She starts wearing pumpkin sweat-

ers as soon as fall rolls around, and probably has no clue what her kids are doing online.

3. **Helicopter Harriet:** This mom hovers and makes comments on every post her kids make. She writes things like "Johnny, why didn't you get an A on that test?" on their walls. Harriet doesn't realize that her comments are embarrassing and can potentially affect her kids' social life and how they make friends.

Each persona was then described further. How old are they? Are they involved in the PTO? Do they watch *Modern Family*, or *Family Guy* on TV?

Once Kathryn had a good idea of how each persona lived her life, she knew how to talk to her. Then she created different content that spoke to each top Mom Blogger using the persona archetypes, and 49 out of 50 agreed to review the book. It was a big success and she was featured on television, radio and in *Woman's Day* magazine for the effort.

Do you see how this simple exercise could help you get a better handle on your target audiences? Once you have a clearer picture in your mind of who the individuals are in your audience and what motivates them, the better you'll become at conversing with them. That familiarity helps you create content that moves people to action.

Most businesses don't develop personas in traditional media marketing. They often lump their ideal audiences into broader demographics, and try to generalize their content to appeal to a wider group of people. Why? Because traditional media is used to broadcast—not converse. Kathryn could easily fit all of her personas into a general demographic as far as age, income level and family status. However, social isn't broadcast media. By delving deeper into each personality, she is able to converse with each of them in a much more personal way. This is essential in developing social media content, because the types of conversation and content that resonates with Helicopter Harriet may not mean a thing to Pumpkin Sweater Peggy. It must be crafted so that the person actually thinks you are talking directly to them.

Kathryn's example is a good one if your product is being marketed directly to consumers. However, the same principles apply if you're marketing your products to business owners as well.

For example, if you have a business that caters to the C-suite executive, you still need to know more about them than just the fact that their title is CEO, CIO or CFO (and this applies to all types of marketing content, not just social media).

Direct response copywriters, for instance, learn early about the value of getting into the prospect's head as an individual, whether they're writing a direct mail sales letter or a white paper that will be used for lead generation online.

For example, one of Apryl's specialties is writing white papers. By asking detailed questions of a white paper client who wants to write a thought-leadership piece on data management aimed at CIOs, she's able to find out more about the executive's personality and can build a persona for target marketing similar to Kathryn's as outlined below:

Business to Business (B2B) CIO Persona Example

In a general demographic sense, CIOs are generally male, aged mid-forties to late fifties, with a higher income bracket (over $100k). But that's not really enough to write copy that gets his attention. So Apryl digs a little deeper and finds out more about what drives the ideal target whom she names **Multitasker Mike:**

- Mike's ultra-busy, with lots of irons in the fire; generally works a 60-hour week
- He has a technical background, so he knows what's under the hood, but has to manage groups now and provide answers to the CEO, so priorities have changed

- He's been burned before by going out on a limb, so he's a consensus builder
- He's often frustrated that his department is perceived as a cost center, and he needs to prove his value to the company
- He is required to have all the IT answers at his fingertips, but often butts heads with the CFO, who holds the purse strings
- He's actively looking for new ways to make data management more efficient, yet is cautious about jumping at the next shiny new toy without quantifiable evidence that it works

Knowing these kinds of personality traits and motivators can vastly improve the quality of your content and conversation.

Another trick Apryl learned from one of today's most respected direct response marketers, Clayton Makepeace, is to take some time with the information she's learned about her target market and put herself in their shoes. She might take a few moments to close her eyes, sit back, and imagine:

> "If I were Mike—what would my day look like when I arrive at the office? What's my attitude? I've got a deadline over my head to provide some answers, a meeting with the IT team at noon, and one of my mid-level managers is dragging his feet in compiling the data we need. Meanwhile the CFO just left me an urgent message—he's breathing down my neck… I can feel my stress level rising (reaching in my desk drawer for that half-empty bottle of antacids).
>
> What's next? What information can I get that will provide those answers in a hurry? I'd better be able to get everyone on board before the next executive briefing or my job is toast!"

By taking this in-depth look at what makes the target CIO tick, she understands that he is probably not interested in a typical sales piece or a data sheet. He's going to need to see in-depth content that includes quantifiable information gathered from sources respected by upper management—with real-world examples of where solutions have worked for similar businesses. He doesn't have lots of time, so content has to grab him where he lives, and it must cut to the chase.

Do you see the importance of taking the time to flesh out your personas? It doesn't matter if your audience is a Social Sally or a Multitasker Mike; without an in-depth look at what motivates them as individuals, you won't be able to make conversation with them, and you'll waste valuable time creating content that won't precisely fit their needs.

Time to Take Action

Right now, take some time to develop one or several personas for your own target market. You might also want to include things like where your persona shops in your local area and then visit those shops and observe the kinds of people who are actually there. Does reality match the persona you made up? Also check out some magazines your target persona may read. Look at the articles and headlines—what types of problems do they address? How do the articles address them?

What are your goals?

Now that you've got the WHO worked out (who your ideal target market is) the next piece of the puzzle is the WHY. Why even use social media? What are you trying to achieve?

Interestingly, this is a tough question for a lot of business owners to answer. Many think they have to use social media because some expert told them to or because they think it will cut advertising costs, because it's "free" after all, right?

This kind of thinking is flawed. Social media should not be viewed as a magic bullet; it's a tool. Like any tool, if it is used properly you can see massive results. The important thing to remember is to make sure that your objectives and strategies for using social media are in sync with your particular audience.

Contrary to popular opinion, your goal should not be just to get tens of thousands of followers on Twitter, or "likes" on your Facebook fan page. Those numbers aren't as important as the relationships you establish.

It's much more desirable to have a few loyal followers who comment, re-tweet and recommend you to their friends than to have thousands who follow you once and then never interact with you again.

In fact, *Nielsen Wire* reports that their research shows 90 percent of consumers surveyed noted that they trust recommendations from people they know, while 70 percent trusted consumer opinions posted online.[2]

Is this really surprising? We ask for recommendations from our friends all the time for plumbers, doctors, day care providers and so on. This was going on long before social media even existed; we'd probably call or email our friends for this information. But now it's even easier. All we have to do is post a question on Facebook or Twitter, or search the Internet for blogs and review sites like *Yelp*, *TripAdvisor* and *Angie's List* to help us make decisions.

People don't give out recommendations lightly. Trust is a big issue online, so you want to outline goals that include creating long term relationships with your customers so they pass on the good news to their friends and followers.

Now Let's Talk About the WHY for Your Business

Different businesses have different goals in mind for using social media, but we find that the objectives seem to fall into four general categories:

1. **Brand awareness:** Simply put, you want as many people as possible to know about you, your brand and your products or services. Social media lets you be in more places online than just your website, and have a presence in places where lots of people are gathering. By being "out and about" and active in the online community, you can develop visibility that stretches beyond your advertising reach through the power of conversation and sharing.

2. **Customer service:** You probably know it's easier to keep a customer than convert a new one. Social media lets you take customer service to a higher level by reacting in real time to customer complaints and compliments. A good social media monitoring plan (covered in Step Six) can help you moni-

tor your online reputation. Often disgruntled customers just want to be heard, and happy customers like to be recognized for positive feedback.

3. **Increasing website or blog traffic:** Everyone loves getting lots of website traffic, and social media platforms are outposts that can drive more visitors to your website. However, getting lots of visitors won't help you if there isn't much relevant content for them to read, watch or hear once they get there.

   People look up your website from social channels to dig deeper—find out more about you. This is where having a company blog on your site can really help. Many people don't think of the blog as part of their overall social media strategy, but it is a huge part. In fact, many top social media experts say that the blog should be the hub of all social media activity. Because people don't like to be "sold" on social media sites, if you drive them back to your blog, which should be housed on your website, then they get to know more about you and perhaps be more likely to purchase your services.

More specifics on blogging later, but here are five steps on plugging your blog into your overall social media strategy:

1. Write a blog post
2. Post updates on Facebook and Twitter with teasers about your new blog post (people click the link to go and read it)
3. Send a teaser about your blog post in your email newsletter (people click the link to go read it)
4. People comment on your blog post and share your link so even more people come to your blog
5. Interact with your followers on all the different platforms (blog, Facebook, Twitter, etc.) and they get to know, like and trust you

Of course, you should also post daily social media updates on other topics besides your blog; however, the bulk of your online community should be aware of your blog and visit it regularly.

Keep in mind that most people don't like to share blatant sales pitches. Messages that have a blog post attached that can offer a solution to one of your client's problems will get shared more and can lead to the last broadly defined goal of social media marketing:

4. **Client acquisition:** Why do we leave this for last? Because social media is NOT a place for sales first; it's an online networking opportunity—a place to build a community.

What if you showed up at an in-person networking event and walked up to everyone saying "Hi, I'm so-and–so, and my product is the best; you should buy it!" before establishing any rapport? No one appreciates that kind of approach. The same is true for social media, which is really online networking.

Re-Think Your Approach

Social channels are for two-way communication. Talk to people and let them talk to you. Post things they're interested in. Let them know that you understand their pain points and that you or your product can address them in a natural way.

Before social media, we used communications like direct mail and email, hoping the recipients get to know you and like you and eventually become a customer. However, those are one-way communications, and you either have to buy (rent) a list of recipients (as in direct-mail lists), or develop a house email list of your own (which can take years).

Using social media as a two-way conversation starter gives you a stronger opportunity to connect than any one-way medium. Does that mean you can throw out your mailing lists if you use social? Absolutely not! Email is still one of the most valuable resources you have for staying in front of your customers.

Instead, use social media as a foot in the door, and a way to organically grow your in-house mailing list. People are much more likely to trust you with their email or mailing address if they've had a chance to get to know you and have found your content valuable.

Here are a few examples of how other organizations have successfully navigated the social space to grow their businesses:

A Dental Practice:

Michael Sinkin, DDS from New York, tells us how he used social media to reach out and build relationships with a younger, more digital audience.

> About 20 years ago, I bought my practice from a dentist who was retiring. It was a very healthy practice and I was busy all the time for many years treating the original patients and also growing a new, younger patient base (albeit slowly for the latter).
>
> About three years ago, I realized that I needed to start to reach a younger audience to keep the stream of new patients growing as my older patients were...um, disappearing. One of my close friends (also a patient) recommended that the best way to achieve this was to use social media.
>
> I was also dismayed that when I Googled my own name, all I saw were listings from sites such as *Healthgrades*, which I had no control over. I saw nothing that told my story the way I wanted it told to potential patients. I am very aware that when someone is referred to a dentist, that person will do online research before they ever make a call to the office for an appointment. I wanted people to be able to see why I am the right choice, and not have to hunt for information about me.

So I hired a local social media consultant and put together a plan. We wanted to reach people in their late 20s to early 50s, who are employed and who live in New York City. We also added a second demographic; all of the above, plus those who work or live near my office, which is located just south of Grand Central Terminal.

We created a Facebook page and a Twitter profile. We decided to use Twitter as the main focus because it is easy to connect with people who fit my desired demographic. I created signs in my office asking people to "Like" my Facebook page and to follow me on Twitter. Meanwhile, my consultant began engaging with people on Twitter, especially those who were complaining of tooth problems, or actually said "Need a Dentist!"

The community began to build. It was amazing! Within the first few months I began to get calls from new patients who said that they had seen one of their Twitter friends talking about me. From then on, I got one or two new patients per month solely from Twitter. Now that may not seem like a lot for many businesses, but it's significant to me because my experience is this: most of my patients stay with me for many, many years, and they also refer me to their friends and family. So each new patient is a source of revenue over the long term.

So what do I tweet about? Well, a key to what I do is my blog. My blog is a combination of stories about my patients, my practice, and a bit of my signature pontificating.

Interspersed within all that are tips and answers that are really helpful for anyone having a dental emergency or just needing information. For example, my blog post, "5 Ways to Get Relief for a Toothache" has been re-tweeted 37 times and counting!

What have I learned from my experience using social media?

I have learned that using social media effectively can be very time-consuming. I need my consultant to help me

> stay on track. I don't have a lot of time and she is always right on top of me to approve a blog or to answer an online question. And staying focused on one or two platforms instead of spreading myself thin works for me.
>
> I don't offer "specials" and don't want to compete with the large dental "salons" and cosmetic dentistry "factories" in my dental practice. Good, positive information about what patients can expect when they see me is very powerful. And because of Twitter, my blog, and Facebook, when someone Googles me now, I'm confident that what they see is what I want them to see.
>
> Also, it doesn't hurt that I have a great sense of humor and am never at a loss for words!

At this writing, Dr. Sinkin has over 4,000 followers on Twitter, his main social media platform for connecting with patients, and his regular blog posts consistently get shared by readers.

Another great example of small business success using social media is:

Hyper Martial Arts, a Martial Arts Clothing Retailer

Jason Morgan, VP of Marketing and Sales for Hyper Martial Arts, tells us how he uses social media to reach a largely teenage audience online.

> Hyper Martial Arts is a youth action sports clothing store, and our demographic is teens and youth age 13-17, and 18-24, interested in Martial Arts, Tricking, Taekwondo and Karate. Interestingly, our audience is largely (67%) female.
>
> We're a small business start-up (founded in 2009), with just six people in the organization, and our sales are derived online and from over 50 retail partner stores in the US, with more in Canada, Europe and Australia.

Most of our online sales are driven from social media (specifically Facebook and Twitter), which gives us high traffic to our website with virtually no advertising spend.

We started out on Facebook, using ads with a low budget ($10 a day in ads the first year), and our focus was to appeal to our demographic with lots of great visuals and content, consistent branding and a non-salesy, interactive approach. First, we developed relationships with 11 of the top young martial arts youth athletes (Pros).

We created training videos with each Pro for a "signature series" that was housed on our Facebook page. From there we created content for each Pro to share on their own social platforms. We also encourage Pros to shoot their own videos and share on the Hyper wall.

We also partner with martial arts schools, distributors and other organizations for events, which create more interest. Events seem to drive pretty high fan counts and interaction.

Another thing we do is curate other people's content from blogs, other martial arts sites and sports sites. We also have had great success leveraging video and photos (both producing our own and asking others to share on our wall).

We employ a flexible, 11-week editorial calendar based on upcoming events, pro content and weekly engagement, which includes fun reasons to visit the page, such as:

a. Monday—Weekly pro spotlight feature

b. Tuesday—Product spotlight

c. Wednesday—World-wide check-in

d. Thursday—Throw-back Thursday (post old martial arts videos)

In a nutshell, our strategy is to use Facebook mainly for content built around Pros (we use our blog more for events/contests/pro guest-posts). Twitter helps us there as well.

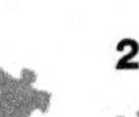

Social gives us a way to provide excellent customer service, and we stay top of mind with immediate interaction and feedback. I spend about two hours a day curating content, posting and interacting on the Facebook wall and via Twitter, and those efforts have paid off, with over 60,000 fans, and more than $10,000 in clothing sales attributed to social over the last year.

What lessons have I learned?

1. It's important to measure your efforts. We use tools like *Google Analytics* and *Facebook Insights* to keep track.
2. Honesty, transparency and consistent branding and voice are also important. Always be thinking of providing value.
3. Be flexible! You never know when a platform will change, so be ready to take advantage of new things. For instance, when the Facebook platform did an overhaul, we reached out to friends in the community for expertise to help us get on top of it.

What's next for Hyper? We're looking into developing an iPhone app to help us reach out to even more followers and friends.

These are two good examples of how retail and consumer services have incorporated social into their marketing plans. But social media isn't limited to consumer markets. If your target market is other businesses, you can still use social media effectively. Here is a great example of a B-2-B company that has experienced success with social media marketing:

Garrett Smith, CMO of VoIP Supply

A leading "Voice over IP" solutions provider in North America, outlines his company's social media success journey.

Social media has been a catapult to my career. When I first started at VoIP Supply in 2005, I was a recent college grad. I started out as a commission-only sales rep, eventually climbing into a marketing role with the company.

Back then we had virtually no budget, but blogging was just starting to take off, and I was really excited about getting into it. I made a proposal to the CEO, and said "I really want to get into corporate blogging, and would like to write a post on the top 30 bloggers in the VoIP industry. What do you think?"

He thought about it, and came back with, "Not sure that's appropriate for our company right now, but go ahead and do it on your own."

Early Blogging Days

So I launched "Smith on VoIP." Here I was, in my early 20s, with no authority, no experience… but I wrote articles that covered everything I knew about VoIP. I wrote every day, and commented on other people's posts and shared links.

All of a sudden a major blogger in the space sent me an email that said "Who are you??" So I opened a dialog and made a connection—sort of got the whole thing rolling. After doing this for about six months, I had accumulated about 200 articles, and decided to go ahead and float my original blog idea (the one I approached the CEO with) of writing about the top 30 bloggers in the space.

After posting that article, a remarkable thing happened. Virtually everyone on that list linked back to my blog—and other blogs linked back—and I got a flood of emails coming in. I was invited to industry trade shows and built lots of relationships; it's amazing how things really started to roll. So we decided to start the corporate blog, "VoIP Insider" in 2006, and I continued to write for both.

Branching into Social

Our company was also an early adopter of Twitter, although we don't count followers as a rule. In B-2-B, our customers want access to information that will help them make better business decisions, so we use Twitter to share that type of content. Our Twitter strategy was (and still is) primarily to provide thought leadership. I wrote e-books and product guides, and spent three months writing guides for all our major product sectors. We also did some paid search, organic SEO and event marketing—and early on we linked our Twitter account to our e-commerce web platform so people could get immediate updates when new products came out. That was huge.

Today we use a multi-faceted approach with Facebook, LinkedIn, Twitter and Google+, in addition to some off-shoot sites. However, providing good content is still our mainstay, and all my staff members have personal blogs. We train them to write by giving them the space to write about their kids, their dog—personal stuff they like and are comfortable talking about. Once they're comfortable there, they'll be more natural at blogging for the organization.

Company Content Philosophy

Our philosophy from the beginning was to always add value before asking people to do business with us, and it has really paid off. We went from no budget for content and communications (with me as the sole writer), to a budget of around $20K a month. We now have multiple freelancers who write for us, and a dedicated marketing communications firm to work with blogger relations, e-books, and a small amount of social ads. But our premise has always been first and foremost, to supply thought leadership, education, knowledge and expertise. That's very important for our business, because we sell what others sell—and that's how we differentiate ourselves. We continue to publish content on an expert level.

Last year we created what I call the "A Team." This is a lead group of internal associates who get a crash course in the fundamentals of writing, social etiquette and online networking. If they show an aptitude for that, we move them into some intense HTML training, basic SEO, how to write blog posts and e-books, and how to integrate good content in the sales cycle.

My goal for the "A-Team" is to create an army of Garrett Smiths in our company, because social permeates everything we do in the organization, and it needs to be done right.

Pitfalls to Avoid

There are a few mistakes I see B-2-B companies make when integrating social:

1. **Limping in:** Dipping a toe in the water to see what happens doesn't get you anywhere. You need a dedicated drive or you won't be successful. Today the barriers to success in social media are higher than when we started—there's no more first mover advantage—so you need to go in strong.
2. **Too Closely Guarded:** Many B-2-B companies still produce dry, boring technical manuals that are like eating a shoe; they're hard to digest. You need to be more customer-centric. People want easy-to-absorb information before making a buying decision. Social is a great vehicle for this, but companies still talk features and functions instead of leading someone by the hand and asking how they can help.
3. **How Come No-one Bought?** People often confuse "direct marketing" with "direct communication." They're two different things. Social is "direct communication," and is the fastest, easiest way to communicate with people in their favorite environment. If someone sends you a message in Facebook, respond

to them in kind (on Facebook). Social is NOT a one-way messaging/advertising system that's tied to an automatic sale. Just because you created a profile on a platform, doesn't mean people will suddenly buy from you. You need to build customer experience and brand awareness first. The needle doesn't move directly—it moves indirectly—from an accumulation of effort in everything you're doing socially.

4. **Outsourcing Too Much:** There are some things, like social strategy, training and education that you can outsource effectively. However, I don't think you should outsource your social media interactions with customers and prospects. That should remain in-house, because that communication needs to be authentic. People want to talk to you as a person—someone who is behind the business—not some outside arm that knows nothing about the inner workings of your organization. Marketing is who you are as a company, and outsourcing your company voice is often off-putting in social circles.

What are Some Must-Haves for B-2-B Companies in the Social Space?

1. **Talk to Your Customers:** Ask them questions. What publications do you like to read? What blogs do you follow? What social platforms do you like? You need to get a flavor for where your ideal audience likes to get information, and where they like to just hang out. Go ask your current customers. Once you have that knowledge, you'll be better able to pick the right social platform for your business. For instance, Twitter and LinkedIn are better for our customers, so we spend more time there than on Facebook.
2. **Have a Profile on EVERY Social Platform:** You need some sort of presence in any place a customer

might look for you; because you don't know where things will be going six months from now (we all thought MySpace was going to live forever, didn't we?). So take the time to sign up for new platforms, even if you don't plan to do much with them just yet. At least mark your spot. Things may make a shift but you'll be ready.

3. **Stay on Top of Trends:** Once something becomes a commodity, it's much harder to get attention and compete for market share, so keep your hand on the pulse of what's going on around you. First movers are already dominating most markets, so stay on top of new ones, and dedicate time to learning new technologies every week. For instance, we're trying out Pinterest, even though its demographic isn't really our target market. However, we're finding that it's opening up a new customer base and generating a few leads.

My advice is to keep an eye on emerging trends like you do your stock portfolio. Regular investments will make it grow!

What's new for VoIP?

We're pushing into video now for things like product overviews and how-to productions—and we've worked up to publishing about 1,500 videos online. It's the wave of the future! We recruited some interns to help us build it out, and they've done a fantastic job.

We're also working on ways to manage all the data that our social efforts are generating. What can we do with all these new insights that can make a bigger impact on the organization? How can we better utilize social analytics? These are questions we need to answer to stay ahead of the curve and predict trends in the marketplace, so we're working on getting a better handle on that internally.

Connecting It All Together

When you have your website, blog and social media networks all working together, you get communication flowing in both directions. As the examples of Dr. Sinkin's dental practice, Hyper Martial Arts and VoIP Supply show us, it's quite possible for businesses other than big brands to do well using social media, especially when it's used more as a communication medium than a sales medium. Your success rate really depends on your goals, but with planning and consistency, your social media efforts can indeed bear fruit.

Time to Take Action:

Write down your main goal for social media marketing and why you chose it:

We talked a bit about the blog earlier, and how many people don't include it as part of their social media marketing. However, a well-planned blog can be the foundation of your deep content—your information hub. Your blog feeds your social platforms with content, and they (in turn) point visitors back to your blog. You can easily see its relationship to your social platforms in the diagram below:

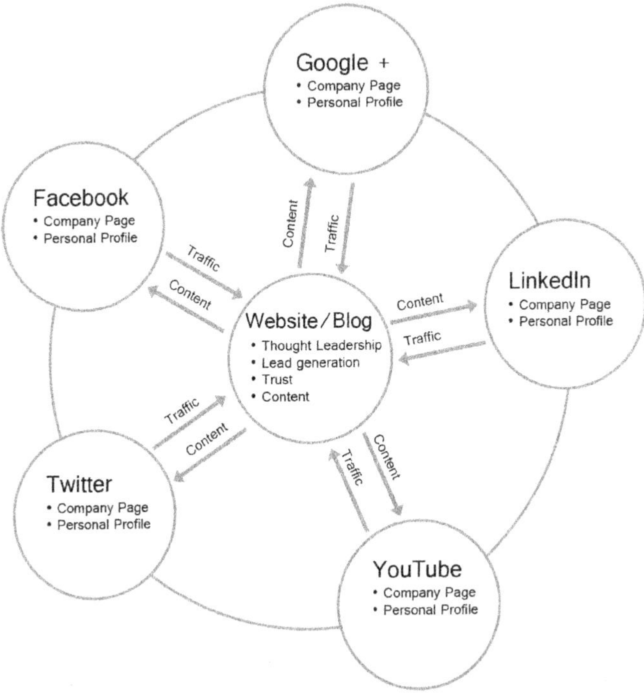

What Kinds of Content Work Best on Blogs?

Lots of people have difficulty thinking about populating a blog. It seems like such a daunting task, especially if you're like most business owners and you're stretched for time. We remember when we first started out. It was really tough to get past that "blank page" syndrome (what the heck do I write about?). So if you're just beginning, here are some of the most popular post types to get you started:

- **Answer common questions:** Make a list of 20 questions you think people would want to know about you or your business and answer one per post. For example, we often get asked about how to build a fan base for Facebook, so one of our posts might be titled "How to build a Facebook Fan Base."
- **Lists: People love lists.** They're short, easy to read, and provide quick information. Stand at any grocery checkout counter and you'll see the magazine headlines: "Top 10 Ways to Lose Belly Fat," "Top 5 Ways to Get Killer Abs," Everyone knows the key to losing weight is to put down the donuts and get off the couch, but we keep buying the magazines thinking there really might be only 10 steps!
- **Interview complementary service providers:** This is really easy. Just email some interview questions to a complementary service provider in your niche and post the Q&A on the blog. As an example, for this book we contacted some of the top influencers in the social media space and asked them to provide content. We sent each an email with five questions and asked them to comment. You can do the same with your business. You can post answers verbatim (e.g., Five Questions with the Expert) or write blog posts around them.

- **Ask others to guest blog for you:** Obviously, you don't want the competition blogging for you. But perhaps you have people that work for your company who can contribute blog posts that answer questions pertaining to their area of expertise. You might also have vendors or other service providers who would be happy to contribute relevant posts. For example, a ski shop could solicit articles from their product manufacturers, ski instruction trainers or physical therapists that are helpful to their audience.
- **Write a commentary on other people's articles or blog posts:** Make sure you give credit to the original source and a link back to the original post by saying something like, "A research study by Forrester was released today that included some interesting findings on companies adopting social media strategies. My take-aways..." and give them a list in bullet points.

Another great way to create content for your blog is by "vlogging" (video blogging). Every post doesn't have to be written. Some people prefer to read, while some prefer to listen—and some like to absorb content visually. There are some blogs that are purely visual, such as *Business Online TV*, but your decision doesn't have to be either-or. Incorporate as little or as much of any style as you like. Mix it up! A written blog can easily be repurposed into a vlog, and now you have two pieces of content.

To make it easy to find things to blog about, Google™ provides a free service called *Google Reader*, which allows you to subscribe to different blogs and online articles by keyword or publication type. You can select to receive an email with new articles about topics in your niche, or view them within the *Google Reader* tab. This way your posts can always be timely and relevant.

Keep in mind, however, that generally blog readers don't want to read thousands of words of content. Posts that are short, concise and to-the-point will get you more readers.

There are lots of other ways to write posts, but you get the idea. The main thing is to get the content flow going. If you're still overwhelmed, you can hire people to write blog posts for you or use a service that will get you started. We expand more on this in Step Five.

To help you even further, we interviewed a couple of experts in the blogging space. The first is one of the world's most recognized thought leaders on blogging. Denise Wakeman, CEO and founder of the Blog Squad, answers some key questions for us on business blogging:

> **Q:** For small businesses, is there an optimum posting frequency you recommend?
>
> **A:** In my opinion there is no frequency that's optimal for all small businesses. It depends on the audience as well as the commitment and resources of the business. That being said, more frequent posting usually translates to more traffic and more traffic will generate more leads.
>
> Typically I recommend posting two to three times per week, if possible. At a minimum, posting once a week is recommended in order to ensure fresh content for visitors, maintaining a stream of traffic and establishing a body of content that demonstrates expertise and thought leadership in the niche.
>
> **Q:** What suggestions do you have for getting other people to "guest blog" for you? Are there pitfalls to avoid?
>
> **A:** First, add a page to your blog with a form to make it easy for potential guest bloggers to submit their articles. This will be more efficient for both the publisher and the guest blogger.
>
> Second, make sure your guidelines are very clear. You'll still get a lot of irrelevant articles, but it will help eliminate

the spammers. Make sure you're very clear about the type of content you're seeking.

Ask for a link to a blog or website so you can check out the author and make sure they are legitimate. There are a lot of people who ghost write for others merely to promote their products. The articles serve as ads and generally do not offer much value. Don't be afraid to say "no" to more articles than you accept. After all it's the reputation of your blog and your business on the line.

Third, let everyone in your circles know you are soliciting guest posts. Post the link to the submission page on your Facebook page, Twitter, LinkedIn groups, Google+ and any other social networks on which you're active.

Q: Do you have tips on the best strategies for putting together an editorial calendar?

A: There are two steps to creating an editorial calendar. First is to assign your blogging to time slots when you know your creative juices are flowing, when you typically feel inspired and productive. For me, that's usually in the morning.

To build a body of content that is quickly indexed by the search engines, I suggest writing on your blog two to three times a week. So block that time off—for example: Monday, Wednesday, Friday from 9:00 to 9:30 am is blogging time. That's the time you spend writing.

Make a list of categories that are of interest to your audience. Take a look at your categories and make a list of 5 to 10 subtopics that relate to each category. If you have 10 primary categories and 5 subtopics for each category, you have 50 blog posts at your fingertips.

Next, assign each subtopic idea to a date on your editorial calendar. Now you've got four months of blog post ideas so you're not facing a blank page.

Finally, two days a week, spend 30 minutes reading other blogs in your industry and leaving comments where appropriate when you have something of value to add.

Not only does that help give you more visibility and more exposure, it also can drive traffic back to your own blog. It positions you as being active and brings you to the attention of other people who you might not have known before.

Q: What resources do you recommend for syndicating blog content?

A: Syndication refers to the efficient distribution of your content across the Web, generally using your RSS feed to do so. First I recommend that you get your blog content syndicated on the major social networking sites where you participate: Twitter, LinkedIn and Facebook. A caveat with Facebook, though, is that you don't get as much exposure with automated syndication, so I recommend you manually post your articles on Facebook.

Results from periodic surveys reveal that Facebook tends to be among the most effective sources of traffic to blogs. Twitter and LinkedIn follow. Google+ is also critical for syndication as it's been shown to help with search engine optimization.

Next, consider participation in communities that promote sharing content. Two of the most popular are Social Buzz Club and Triberr.

As for tools, there are hundreds of tools to automate Twitter syndication. A few include: TwitterTools (a

WordPress plugin), Twitterfeed, Hootsuite, SocialOomph, and Buffer.

Probably most important is including social sharing buttons on all of your blog posts. This encourages and makes it easy for your readers to amplify your content to their communities. Sharing tools we recommend are Digg Digg and Sexy Bookmarks. There are hundreds of plugins to help you do this, so pick one that complements the look and feel of your site.

Our second expert is Hollis Gillespie, Humorist, NY Times Best Selling Author and Owner of the popular *Shocking Real Life Writers Academy*. We asked Hollis to offer her advice on blogging, particularly for those who are just starting out.

Q: How often should you post?

A: For a new blog, you should post once a day for the first 30 days in order to provide content and generate an audience — also, you need to give Google material to put you on their search-result pages. After the first 30 days, you should post at least 3—5 times a week. Your audience wants to see new material when they check back in, and if your new posts aren't there, you will lose loyalty very quickly. Keep those new posts coming and your audience will grow steadily.

Q: If you're new to blogging, how do you draw traffic to your posts?

A: One way is to use *Google Trends* to help you discover "what's hot," so you can create posts that are more likely to draw readership. Let's say Lindsay Lohan got arrested again for drunk driving, and her name is at the top of the trending list. And let's say you write a consumer blog about cars. "The Car So Safe Even Lindsay Lohan Can Drive It," would be an example of how you can twist that

> trending topic to your favor. It's a cheap, but very effective device to drive traffic to your site.
>
> Also, isolate your content to specific niches and avoid trying to be everything to everybody—a common mistake with new bloggers.
>
> If you want to monetize your blog, it's all about finding your niche. The kitchen-sink approach doesn't work on the web. You have to be very, very specific. If you want to write a blog about dogs, pick a specific breed. If you want to [blog] about food, pick a specific kind; the more specific the better (e.g., Gluten-free? Deep-fried candy bars?). Your audience is global now. Out of the six billion people on the planet, you will attract enough who are as passionate as you are about this one specific subject.

Denise and Hollis shared some thought-provoking ideas on how to approach blogging, especially for those just starting out or who would like to get more out of their blogging efforts. For many people the hardest part is planning the content. Thinking up the first few topics isn't that hard—but how do you multiply that out without running out of things to talk about?

Another blogging expert, Chris Garrett, uses a simple tool brainstorm topics. He uses a "spinoff" diagram. This is a simple diagram of a big circle, surrounded by five smaller circles that helps to map out content for your blog. Below is an example that Apryl used for one of her clients, a ski retailer:

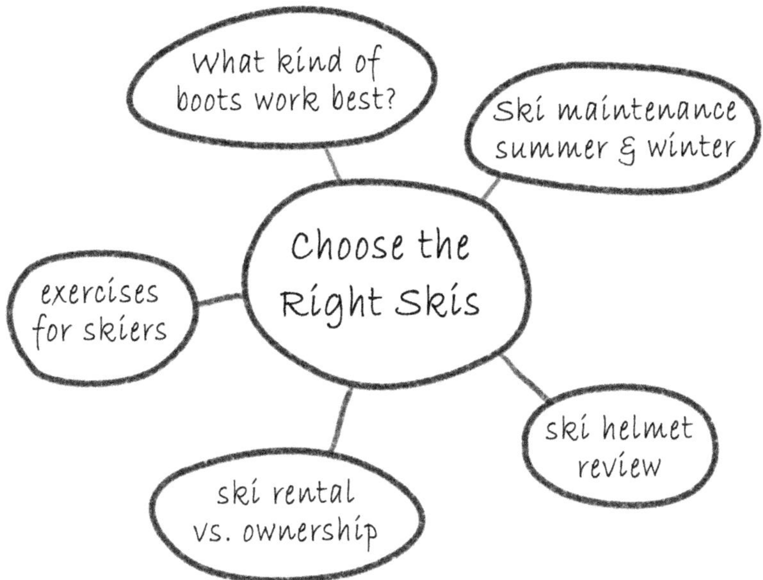

In the largest circle, write the title of a topic you would like to address. Then on each of the smaller circles, think of a tangent topic—one that's related to the main topic, but could be a good spinoff post. Chances are you can think of at least five for any one major topic. Do this for five main topics, and violá! You have 25 blog post ideas.

Time to Take Action:

Take a moment and write down the top 20 questions people ask about your business. These questions will give you a good start on some blog topic ideas, and will likely spawn some creative thinking for even more posts.

Step Four: Choosing the Right Social Networks

Now that you have the WHO (target market) and the WHY (why am I here), and the beginnings of a blogging strategy which will serve as the "hub" of your activity, it's time to decide the WHAT. What networks will you use? After establishing the deep content that will hold your customer's interest, it's time to explore social platforms.

The Big 5 Social Networks

There are literally thousands of social networks to choose from. However, this section explores five of the most heavily used social networks: Facebook, Twitter, LinkedIn, YouTube and Google Plus.

On each platform we'll start out with some overall statistics for each network, followed by expert advice from other respected social media professionals on how to best integrate the platform into your overall marketing strategy.

FACEBOOK

Information taken from an infographic published by *OnlineMBA.com*[3]

- Facebook has over 850 million active users
- The average Facebook user has 130 friends

- The average Facebook visit lasts 23 minutes
- 46% of Facebook users are over the age of 45
- 57% of Facebook users are female (43% male)
- 57% of Facebook users report having been to "some college" (24% bachelors or graduate degree)
- 47% of Facebook users report making between $50,000 – $99,000 annually (33% between $25,000 – $49,999)

With over 850 million users and climbing, Facebook is now used by one in every 13 people on earth, and over 250 million of them (over 50 percent) log in every day. Interestingly, 40 percent of those follow brands, and they interact with the brand through their personal news feed. However, that doesn't mean they'll necessarily see your posts. In fact, Facebook uses an algorithm called "Edgerank" to determine whether or not your page's posts will even make it to the news feeds of your fans.

Why Edgerank Matters

The Edgerank algorithm is largely a mystery but understanding at least some of it is critical to your Facebook strategy success. In fact, a survey conducted by the blog *Allfacebook.com* and *Edgerankchecker.com* on over 4,000 Facebook pages found that only 17% of those pages' fans ever saw their content in their newsfeeds.[4] That's a one in six ratio!

The purpose of EdgeRank in Facebook's words is "to aggregate content that a person will find interesting. It displays stories based on their relevance rather than in chronological order."

What do we know about Edgerank? We know that Facebook ranks your status updates, pictures, and videos (Facebook calls all of these "objects") based on three factors: Affinity, Weight and Time Decay.

Affinity refers to the number of times fans interact with your page content and how often you interact with your fans.

Weight is given to posts by users sharing, commenting or liking your posts. Facebook ranks posts shared more highly because if a user shares your post, it goes to their friends as well. That means it could potentially be seen by hundreds, even thousands of other users (many of whom probably are not fans of your page).

Commenting gets the middle amount of weight for the algorithm, and "likes" get the least; however, likes are still very important. Anytime fans interact with your page, you get scored higher.

Time decay is exactly what it sounds like. More recent posts are more likely to get featured. Facebook wants new content (and so do your fans).

Another thing that helps your posts show up more readily in users' news feeds is the update type. Facebook loves posts with "media" (photos, videos); include these in your content regularly and it will be scored higher. The next highest level is posts with links attached, and the third are regular status updates.

What does this tell us? Be consistent and post content that will encourage interaction and you will catch the attention of not only your fans but Facebook as well.

You can do your own calculation to see how your page is doing. Look at your Facebook Insights, average the reach of your last ten posts, and divide that by your total fan count.

Another reason to post relevant and engaging content instead of just coupons and deals is that while many people will follow a brand to receive deals and discounts, over 40% of a brand's Facebook page fans "unlike" the page as soon as an advertising/engagement campaign ends.[5]

The blog *Emarketer.com* cited a survey conducted by *DDB Paris* and *OpinonWay*,[6] which revealed that two in five brand followers surveyed were not interested in engaging with Facebook pages after a marketing engagement ends, and 49 percent of those who clicked the "unlike" button said the reason they did so was that, "The brand was no longer of interest to me."

Other reasons cited by the survey respondents:

- The information available was not interesting (46%)
- Information was published too often (36%)
- The brand published information I did not appreciate (27%)
- Information was not published often enough (14%)

So readers, put yourself in your fans' shoes. Have you "unliked" a Facebook brand page? Was it for any of the reasons mentioned above?

What does all this information tell us? Facebook's reach for most target markets is huge, and for that reason alone, it's one of the most popular social channels for business. However, with its sheer volume of traffic and its Edgerank algorithm it can be a bit challenging for brands to "get heard." Plus, as mentioned earlier, studies show that even if you are successful in getting someone to like you or your brand, that doesn't mean they will stick around. People interact with content, not coupons. If you are giving your audience valuable information that you know they need (from your persona creation) you will be less likely to experience the "unlike" after a campaign is over.

Also, the blog *Allfacebook.com* shared that people go to your page one time to like it and then never return. They interact with you from their newsfeed. Most people are only interested in the newsfeed—that's all Facebook is to them.[7] In light of this, your content must remain interesting in order for people to consistently see your brand messages.

Because of the personal nature of the network and the vast number of users, Facebook is great for meeting objectives such as brand awareness, customer service and blog traffic generation. You can delete comments you don't want on your wall and push messages you want people to see, so, in many ways you control the message. Facebook also has very flexible and highly targeted advertising options (more on that later).

To help you better understand how to get the most from Facebook, we've solicited input from some of today's brightest Facebook marketers. Amy Porterfield, Social media strategist and co-author of *Facebook Marketing All-In-One for Dummies* is first with her advice on how to turn fans into Super Fans.

> **Q:** What are your tips on content that can turn fans into Super Fans?
>
> **A:** Without quality fans, your Facebook marketing efforts can fizzle out quickly. The goal is to move your fans to Super Fan status. Super Fans are Facebook users who have given you access to their data via their Facebook profile, purchased from you and also encouraged another fan to purchase from you as well. There's no doubt we all want an abundance of Super Fans!
>
> So how do you move a potential fan all the way up the ranks to Super Fan? One way to do this is to move your fans to action by creating consistent calls to action on your Facebook page.
>
> To do this, start out by posting valuable content, such as interesting articles and videos related to your niche, and accompany this content with simple calls to action such as "click this" or "watch this." The valuable content will show your fans that you're an authority and consistently post good stuff.
>
> Also, consider offering discounts and specials or ask your fans to sign up for your newsletter. These are all low-investment calls to action that will help you build trust and affinity over time.
>
> Lead the way with free valuable content and later offer opportunities that require more of a commitment from

your fans (such as giving their name and email in exchange for a giveaway or purchasing a product).

Offering free webinars and teleseminars that provide training up front are great ways to promote your programs and services without having to sell too hard on your Facebook page.

Q: What types of content are best to create engagement on Facebook?

A: The key to creating content that will engage your fans is to make it actionable and relevant. Focus on delivering added value to your core market at every opportunity.

Deliver actionable takeaways. Cater to their interests. Remember to educate, entertain AND empower—no matter what topic you're covering.

If you want to educate AND empower your readers, you're going to need to give them evidence that what you're saying or doing really works—and that's where you can go above and beyond your competitors.

Statistics, infographics, research and quotes from experts (especially from a new interview YOU conduct) are great ways to add value and create truly unique content.

Q: What are the most important metrics that brands should watch for on their Facebook page?

A: Facebook isn't just the largest social media networking site on the web (over a billion active users), it also collects a massive amount of information about those users. Through *Facebook Insights*, page owners can access a staggering amount of information about their fans' activities.

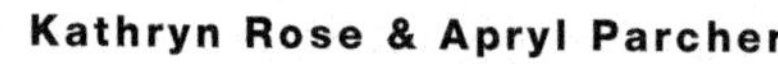

This information gives business owners valuable insight into what they need to do to give fans a better experience and in turn, get better marketing results.

But it can be challenging to sift through all that data. An easy way to avoid metrics overdose is to find and target just a few key metrics.

Below are three game-changing metrics you should be tracking to ensure you are engaging your fans and creating a thriving community of prospective buyers.

People Talking About This

"People Talking About This" is one of the new metrics for Facebook pages and, unlike other metrics on your Insights dashboard, it's also the only one visible to the public.

This number represents the total number of people who, over the past seven days, engaged with your page in any way — by liking it, commenting on or sharing a post, answering a question, tagging your page, or responding to an event. In your Insights dashboard, you'll also see a percentage increase or decrease next to the current number, so you can compare this week's engagement against last week's stats.

Engaged Users

On your Insights dashboard, you'll see a chart in the "Page Post Information" area with a column called "Engaged Users." The number represents the number of unique people who have clicked anywhere on that post. (Note: Insights only tracks this for 28 days.) "Engaged Users" is another engagement-related metric, but since it tracks actual clicks, you can see how your audience interacts with your posts, and use this information to craft more engaging calls-to-action.

External Referrers

Click on "Reach" (under Insights in your admin panel) and scroll down to find "External Referrers." You'll see a list showing how many times people arrived on your Facebook page from an external site during the selected date range.

All business owners should know where and how people are finding them online. While it's important to direct traffic from social media to your main "hub," whether it's a blog or a static business site, bringing traffic onto your Facebook page is also important.

Why? Because Facebook allows you to have conversations and build relationships that you just can't have on a regular website. Those conversations can yield powerful market insights and, eventually, lead to actual sales.

Next we asked Laura Rubinstein, President of Social Buzz Club, LLC, & Transform Today, Inc. and creator of the social media *Blast Off* course for business for some thoughts on post timing and creating content that drives engagement.

Q: How do brands get the most out of their posts?

A: I think a combination of things come into play, but timing and type of content are critical:

Timing and Frequency Matter

A study by Toronto-based "Engagement Bar" company *Visibli* revealed that 50 percent of all the Likes that a Facebook post gets occur within the first hour, 70 percent of all the Likes per post happen within the first four hours and 95 percent of all the Likes a post will ever get occur within the first 22 hours.[8]

That's right; within less than a day, the lifecycle of your post is over. That means you need to pay attention to two things, posting often and during peak visibility hours.

I am often asked, "How often should I post to my Facebook fan page?" With Facebook's new design that includes the ticker and the News Feed that shows most popular content first, I am recommending posting at least once a day and as much as five times/day to your fan page. If you can only post once a day, test out posting at different times during the day, then review your insights and compare engagement results.

You may find your target market is online in the morning, during lunch, or after work. Also according to kissmetrics.com, 80 percent of the population of the United States lives in the Eastern and Central time zones.[9] So if you want to make sure they see your posts, consider the timing of your posts in those time zones.

If you're considering scheduling your posts via a third-party scheduling platform (like Hootsuite), you may encounter less engagement from your posts because Facebook penalizes posts that are not shared directly. In other words, your fan page posts may not show up in the news feed for as many of your fans if you use systems like *Hootsuite*, *SocialOomph*, *Emailvision*, etc. I'm not saying not to use them, but keep that in mind as you create your strategy.

Create Compelling Content

You can have the best timing in the world, but if you are not seriously thinking through and strategically developing rich engaging, entertaining or "edutaining" (educating and entertaining) content, then you may be in for a shockingly low engagement rate. So consider your content carefully.

Use Video

Consider crafting edutaining videos on a consistent basis. Videos of you talking may not cut it. If you are unsure what kinds of videos to produce, I recommend checking out your competitors, searching on YouTube for trending content in your industry and brainstorming with a video marketing expert. You may also make personalized videos to your fans and welcome them to your page once a week. Remember to friend them and tag them. As long as you are under the 5,000 friend limit, you may friend more people.

Video is not a must by any means. Although Facebook has increased the character limit on a post to 50,000 characters, the social enterprise company *Buddy Media* came out with some incredible statistics that Facebook posts that were 80 characters or less got a 27 percent higher rate of engagement. My guess is that most of those posts were questions.

Ask Questions

I love asking questions on Facebook pages. It's a great way to learn, get great ideas, generate conversation and engage; however, questions must be crafted carefully. If you ask questions that require a lot of thinking to answer, you may get very little response. Remember, people spend a lot of time on Facebook, but they are quickly going from post to post and page to page. So ask easy-to-answer questions. If they need to think too hard or your question results in a deer-in-the-headlights feeling, you won't get any answers. You may want to ask for feedback or advice on something you're doing (keep it simple).

Q: Another very important aspect of Facebook marketing is responding and acknowledging your fans, correct?

A: Everyone wants to be heard. If a fan takes the time to Like a post or add a comment to your wall, the very least you can do is acknowledge him or her. As you engage with your fans, a relationship is built between you and your fans. As the relationship grows their trust in you grows. It has been proven that fans who post a question or comment are ready to buy. Eighty percent of them will buy when their question is answered and/or comment is acknowledged with a thoughtful response. That's huge.

Q: How about giving your fans perks?

A: People love getting things for free. In addition to your wonderful content, you might consider hosting a contest, doing a livestream webcast or free webinar, or giving away e-books. To do any of these you'll need to spruce up your fan page with some applications.

To host a contest, make sure you use a third party Facebook application. According to Facebook terms you may <u>not</u> use liking a post or page as an entry to a contest. You may use an application that asks them to like the page as part of the process.

Q: Speaking of contests, do you have any advice on using them?

A: Sweepstakes will get you the most amount of entries but the least "interested" fans. Photo contests will get you less entries but more people who are serious about what you have to offer. Video contests are the most difficult for people to participate in, so unless you need video content, I wouldn't recommend running a video contest. There are several applications available that make managing entries and staying in compliance with Facebook's rules very easy. Among them are *WildfireApp, North Social, Strutta, ContestBurner* and *EasyPromo*, to name a few.

Q: Do you have any advice on using Facebook to get people to sign up for your email list?

A: Give away a free ebook, report, white paper, tip series or other content, and make sure you have a way for them to opt-in right from your fan page. You can do this with an app on your page with an opt-in form that promotes your free content. This builds your email list while giving your fans some great perks. You can use custom page builders to do this—such as *TabSite* or *Lujure* (for a full list check out our resources section at the end of this book).

You need great content, great products/services and consistent giving, and you will reap what you sow.

Facebook Summary:

Both Amy and Laura hit the nail on the head when it comes to Facebook—it's all about engagement. The challenge for most businesses is in the act of engaging. How do you get people to both "like" your Facebook page initially (build audience), and then entice them to stick around and interact with you once they've done so (convert to customers)? Hopefully, the best practices we've outlined can help you master that engagement.

Another challenge in working within Facebook is being flexible when changes come down the pike. Sometimes it can seem that just when you've mastered the interface and tools, Facebook jerks the rug out from under you with massive changes to the platform, creating another learning curve. Don't feel badly—everyone's in the same boat. It's even a challenge for the experts!

What's important is to keep in mind the bigger picture of bringing value, sharing insight, and truly connecting with people on an individual basis. That's what will help you use the platform most effectively. If you build a loyal and engaged fan base, the changes that Facebook makes won't matter. Just change the picture sizes or whatever you need to do to comply with the new design. Your fans will continue to engage in spite of Facebook's latest design whim.

In spite of its challenges, the size of its reach, along with the wealth of information available through its "social graph" makes Facebook a great place for brands. It allows them to not only get in front of their audiences, but also to dig deeper and understand who their audience really is and what makes them tick.

The next platform on our list to explore is Twitter. It may not have quite the demographic reach of Facebook, but it's definitely a place where many businesses interact with followers.

TWITTER

Statistics from OnlineMBA.com and Digital Surgeons[10]

- Twitter has 127 million users
- 13% of Internet users also use Twitter
- 54% of Twitter users use Twitter on their mobile devices
- 36% of Twitter users tweet at least once a day
- The average visit on Twitter lasts for 11:50 minutes
- 59% of Twitter users are female (41% male)
- 25% follow a brand
- Twitter generates over 250 million Tweets per day

Twitter is a "micro-blogging" platform where users "tweet" short messages (140 characters or less) to people who follow their profile, and it generates a massive amount of communication online.

While it seems that Twitter has a large audience and lots of conversations going on, a 2009 Harvard study[11] showed that:

- Only 21% of Twitter users are active users
- 34% of Twitter users hadn't tweeted even once
- A whopping 73% of Twitter's users tweeted less than 10 times

What does this tell us? Nearly all of the tweets were coming from about one-fourth of the user base. Power users dominate. However, don't discount the voyeurs. There are lots of people not talking on a regular basis but they are *listening*.

Only 25 percent follow a brand, telling us that Twitter users want to interact with people first, brands second. We're not saying that brands should not have a twitter page, but it's a good idea for the brand to have some kind of personality. Many companies put right in the bio, tweets from "Suzy Smith" community manager. If you are your brand, keep your tweets a good mix of personal and business.

Another way to think about the difference between Twitter and Facebook is this: *Twitter is the headline, Facebook is the whole story.*

Twitter is also great for customer service, because people can reach you easily through @mentions on the network. For brand awareness, it offers real time communication and insight into public conversations. However, Twitter, unlike Facebook, is more like the Wild West; you cannot control the message. It is not possible to delete tweets that say negative or untrue things.

Unlike Facebook, Twitter has no algorithm where it decides who sees your content. People on the network decide who they interact with and how often. Also, unlike Facebook, brands need to Tweet more often to be noticed. We tell our clients that a tweet is like a grain of sand in the ocean. Once you send the tweet, a wave of other tweets come (depending upon how many people you follow) and wash it away. To succeed on Twitter you not only need compelling content (that stays within Twitter's 140 character rules) but you need to post often enough that your content is actually seen.

How do you accomplish this? We asked two of the top twitter experts to give us their advice.

Ted Rubin, a leading social marketing strategist and Chief Social Marketing Officer at Collective Bias gives us his take on building a loyal community of followers on Twitter. He is also co-author of the upcoming book: *Return on Relationship™, Relationships ARE the New Currency—Honor Them, Invest in Them, and Start Measuring Your ROR!*

> If you want to continue to reach your market in this social media age, the marketing focus needs to be on *building relationships,* and metrics need to expand beyond ROI (Return on Investment) to include ROR: Return on Relationship™.
>
> Return on Relationship simply put, is the value that is accrued by a person or brand due to nurturing a relationship. ROI is simple dollars and cents. ROR is the value (both perceived and real) that will accrue over time through loyalty, recommendations and sharing. ROR is used to define and educate companies, brands and people about the importance of creating authentic connection, interaction and engagement with consumers.
>
> Twitter can be an important platform to use to build those relationships for two reasons:
>
> 1. If you are not engaging in your field of expertise on Twitter, you can be sure that someone else is, so don't miss that opportunity and hand it to others.
> 2. If you are not talking about your business, your customers and prospects probably are, and you are not

there to participate, engage, interact, and most important for your business... listen and lead.

My philosophy is that Twitter is a tool that leads into other forms of social sharing. I consider Twitter a place to lay the groundwork where other people pick up things.

Twitter is a seeing medium and a place to build engagement and interaction. It is not a broadcast medium, so it is not about the quantity of people listening at once, but the ability to lay it out there for those whose attention are drawn to what you have to say at any given moment.

Tweet to keep your personal brand on your followers' radar, increase your following, and provide value that keeps followers listening and you top of mind. To accomplish this, send the same tweet often multiple times in a day and send valuable content repeatedly over the course of time.

Periodically check out your followers' sites to find interesting posts and re-tweet (RT) them to show you are paying attention. Ask your team members to send you tweet ideas regularly as well.

Be sure to track your success:

Track Mentions—The major thing you should be tracking in Twitter is mentions of your twitter name. Anytime somebody mentions your name, it's an opportunity to start a conversation and acquire a new high quality follower.

Track Re-tweets—You should also pay close attention to the people who are re-tweeting your tweets. It's obvious that they like your content, otherwise they wouldn't be sharing it.

Where to Start When You Are at Zero

If you are starting at zero, some of the above might seem more challenging, but it's not. Just start with bloggers you have been reading. This is why it's important to read more than just the "a-list" blogs. Find people you think are interesting and just reach out to them. Whether they're bloggers, marketers or brands, they'll be happy to hear from you.

Create a Twitter List

Twitter's "list" feature can be a good tool for reaching out. Create a list called your "inner circle." Anytime somebody mentions or re-tweets you, make a point to add them to that list, and engage with them. Simply creating the list is not going to be enough—start periodic conversations with the people in your lists. Re-tweet their stuff, and look to periodically RT others to get their attention and interact.

Always Remember:

If you think nobody is tweeting about your products or services, think again. If you're not tweeting about your business—someone else is. If you're not setting your own business message on Twitter—someone else is. But more importantly, if you're not listening to what your customers (and potential customers) are saying on Twitter—someone else is, and you are missing an incredibly valuable opportunity to engage and interact.

Another Twitter expert, Rich Brooks, gives us some of his best tips. Rich is president of Flyte New Media, a web design and internet marketing company, and founder of The Agents of Change Digital Marketing Conference.

Q: Many small businesses have limited time resources. Why do you think small businesses should be spending their time on Twitter?

A: I don't believe that all small businesses *should* spend their limited time on Twitter. As with any social media platform, you should engage your customers and prospects where they are. If your audience isn't on Twitter, it's not a good fit.

Q: How many times a day should they target to engage on Twitter to be successful?

A: There's no magic number, but the more active you are, the more visibility you get. I think it's better to focus on creating quality tweets rather than a specific number—tweets that engage and entertain your audience.

Q: What is your advice about what types of things to tweet?

A: For me, I have a personal account (@therichbrooks) and a business account (@flytenewmedia.) In my personal account it's a mix of business and whatever's on my mind, from the weather to the zombie apocalypse. From my business account, it's more focused on what my ideal customer is interested in.

In short, your goal is to provide value with every tweet. That may mean being funny, breaking big news, providing insight or curating content from other sources.

Q: What are some tools small businesses can use to manage their Twitter engagement?

A: I use *TweetDeck* most often, although I've been playing around with *Hootsuite* because of its ability to post to Facebook pages and schedule tweets and updates.

I'm also a big fan of *paper.li,* which creates semi-curated "newspapers" of the people you follow and topics you're interested in.

Q: What is your advice about building a quality following on Twitter?

A: I'm glad you said quality and not quantity. If you're just getting started, use tools like *Wefollow.com* and *Twellow.com* to find influential people in your and your customers' industries. See what they're saying and join the conversation.

The point is Twitter is NOT a numbers game. Be interesting, be engaging, and you'll attract followers.

If you're doing this for business, just make sure you're talking about the right things. In a personal account you can talk about whatever crosses your mind, but if you're doing this for business, keep your audience's interest first and foremost.

Q: Do you have any examples of small businesses who use Twitter effectively?

A: I think Beadin' Path (@beadinpath) does a great job. She shares pictures of beads she's found, or is using, or buying for the store. She's totally engaged her audience.

Twitter Summary:

Ted and Rich make some very good points on using Twitter, and both stress the importance of being engaging and authentic on this platform.

As Rich mentioned, online social media management tools such as *TweetDeck* and *Hootsuite* can help you manage the flow, narrow audience segments and keep an eye on the types of discussions that matter most to you, and there are lots of other Twitter tools available to help you get the most out of the platform.

The biggest downside to choosing Twitter as your main social media touch point is time. A successful Twitter strategy requires your brand to be very active and reactive, constantly reading and posting to stay top of mind with your followers.

One of Twitters biggest strengths, on the other hand, is its huge amount of data volume. The magnitude of data generated by users of the platform makes it a great place to conduct research. Twitter's search tool, *search.twitter.com*, makes it a good place to listen to what people are talking about right now. It's also great for following trends and gathering insights regarding keywords and competitors. We think it's a good idea to at least have a profile on Twitter, even if you don't plan to use it heavily.

Our next platform is LinkedIn, one of the oldest social networks for business people.

LINKEDIN

Statistics from OnlineMBA.com:

- LinkedIn has members in over 200 countries
- LinkedIn has about 150 million registered users
- About half of the members are outside the US
- Executives from all Fortune 500 companies are LinkedIn members
- Higher income levels (many over $100k per year)
- More than half have a higher education degree
- Demographic evenly split between male and female

- 75% of LinkedIn users use it for business purposes
- There are 2 million companies represented on LinkedIn

Nielsen Online says that the demographics of LinkedIn members compares to other major business outlets such as the *Wall Street Journal*, *Forbes* and *Businessweek*.

What does this tell us? This is the network on which to be present for business-to-business services, and for reaching out to the C-suite executive. LinkedIn is most useful for lead generation because many people are on LinkedIn to do business. However, we recommend that you don't primarily reach out to sell things. Join groups and participate in the conversation. Answer (and ask) questions. It's also a great platform for establishing yourself as an expert in your field and in doing so, gain brand awareness for you and your company.

Although LinkedIn is a "closed" community, meaning you generally have to be specifically invited by others to connect with them, it's a great place to expand your network. Think of it as personal one-on-one networking on steroids. When you connect with another person on LinkedIn, you can view their connections and reach out to those who would make good connections for you.

Following personal networking etiquette is essential in this platform, so keep these tips in mind when using LinkedIn:

- Members are generally reluctant to accept invitations to connect from total strangers. Start with people you know and branch out respectfully.
- LinkedIn users hate promotional messages. Don't use your updates to promote yourself frequently. Instead, share and add value.
- Use your picture and your whole name on the platform. You wouldn't refuse to tell people your name at a physical networking event—don't hide it here.

- When one of your connections messages you, answer back promptly. You never know from where the next business-building opportunity will come.
- Don't be a LinkedIn wallflower. Be thorough on your profile and what you make public, so you can be seen and people can tell right away why they should connect with you.
- Use the "giver's gain" philosophy. Give recommendations before you ask for them, and ask connections what a good referral would be for them.

To dig deeper on LinkedIn, we chose two experts on the platform to help give you more information. Our first LinkedIn expert, Neal Schaffer, author of *Maximizing LinkedIn for Sales and Social Media Marketing* and founder of Windmill Networking, gave us his insights into a successful Linkedin strategy:

> **Q:** What are the top mistakes people make in their personal profiles on Linkedin?
>
> **A:** Many people either put too much or not enough thought into their LinkedIn profile. For instance, you are given a professional headline, which is important for SEO as well as trying to catch the attention of others. Some try to dupe the LinkedIn search engine by just placing a bunch of keywords in there or by trying to pitch themselves with a statement like "Ask me for FREE help on how to xxyyzz!" These efforts will only backfire because your headline really creates the first impression that other business people will walk away with.
>
> It's very similar to a networking meeting: What would you put on your name badge? If you start to think about LinkedIn being one huge networking event, you begin to see how you should showcase yourself in your headline as well as rest of your profile.

Another mistake is how many professionals fail to use all of the "real estate" that LinkedIn provides them. Your LinkedIn profile is an Inbound Marketing tool, not your resume! Every past work experience and keyword you enter into your profile just makes you more searchable in the database of professional profiles that is LinkedIn.

Finally, it kills me when I see small business owners and entrepreneurs who fail to include their contact info in their profile. LinkedIn provides you a section at the bottom of your profile called "Contact Settings" specifically for this purpose. You establish a profile trying to attract leads or business opportunities, but how are new people supposed to contact you? The key is to eliminate any hurdles in preventing people from contacting you, so make sure you include some ways in which readers of your profile can easily get in touch.

Q: Why is it important to have a business profile on LinkedIn, and can you offer tips for setting it up correctly?

A: LinkedIn only offers profiles for people. However, LinkedIn has always had, and continues to invest in, its "Companies Directory." Some people might look for service providers or products by searching through profiles, but more and more are turning to the Companies Directory, because with each company you can find out how your Professional Graph overlaps with the people working at that company. Furthermore, Companies is starting to rival even paid services like *Hoovers.com* in terms of the information that it can provide. Finally, just as Profiles have Recommendations, so do Companies–and getting recommendations from business decision makers on your Company Page is a golden investment in your company's future business.

Setting up a LinkedIn Company Page is not rocket science, and it is similar to the concepts I presented when talking about Profiles: Make sure you complete all of the sections so that your company is discoverable when someone might be looking for your product or service.

If there was one bit of additional advice I would add, it would be to start getting your clients, past and present, to recommend your business on your Company Page. In order to do this you will need to create Products and Services pages. Start with one or two that best represent your business and ask your VIP customers to provide a one or two-sentence recommendation. Every recommendation will go out into their news feed, further increasing the chances that others will find out about your Company Page.

Q: Should people belong to groups and how can they use them to their advantage?

A: LinkedIn Groups are the largest public forums on the Internet for professionals. At current count there are more than 1 million groups that exist on LinkedIn, and many have hundreds of thousands of members! There are a tremendous amount of professionals having discussions, sharing news, and connecting through common group membership. Your personal profile is your homepage on LinkedIn, but outside of connecting and contacting other professionals on LinkedIn, groups is where a majority of the engagement takes place–and you'll want to make sure you are where the action is!

The first thing you should do is perform searches for appropriate LinkedIn Groups based on where you think your target customer might lurk. LinkedIn gives you the ability to join 50 groups, and I recommend you join all 50. Joining a group means that you can message other group members–so joining 50 groups will also help you achieve maximum approachability as well as the ability to directly message many that are out of your immediate network.

What do you do after joining 50 groups? Sign up to receive daily or weekly digests and try to join in, or start, a relevant discussion or two on a daily basis. See which groups seem more engaging or are having conversations that are more suitable to your LinkedIn business objectives.

Try to show off your expertise by responding to questions, commenting on discussions to offer unique perspectives, and even calling on the group by asking questions to better understand your target customer base. One or two engagements a day can help trigger relationships that might lead to business as well as help make you more visible in these huge public forums.

Q: Does LinkedIn have any kind of metrics that users should be aware of?

A: LinkedIn metrics are challenging unless everyone in your organization is registering whenever they have someone contact them through LinkedIn that generates a lead or business. That being said, there are two ways of accessing limited metrics from your LinkedIn presence:

1. If you have a paid account, you can gain access to an application called *Profile Stats Pro.* This will show you a complete list of who has accessed your profile as well as how many times you show up in search results as well as profile views. The interesting metric shown here is what keywords are driving others to your profile. If you want to take an SEO approach to your LinkedIn profile, this data might come in handy.
2. The other metrics provided are for the Company Page. Similar to Facebook Insights, LinkedIn provides information on views, clicks, and other basic information to give you an idea as to how your Company Page is "performing."

Our second LinkedIn expert interview is with Viveka Von Rosen, the host of the biggest LinkedIn chat on Twitter: #LinkedInChat. She is also co-moderator of LinkedStrategies, the largest LinkedIn strategy group on the platform, and author of an upcoming book, *LinkedIn Marketing: An Hour*

***A Day* for John Wiley & Sons. Viveka talks about a few more mistakes to avoid, as well as delving deeper into measurement.**

Top mistakes made on LinkedIn

1. **Using the Resume Uploader:** People still think LinkedIn is a resume on steroids, so many just upload their resume and call it good. This is a mistake for two reasons. First of all, the resume uploader – well – sucks! Why? Let's just put it this way, I have worked with well over 1,000 people, either individually or in groups in optimizing LinkedIn profiles and I have had the uploader work exactly one time. The resume uploader is simply not intelligent enough to pull the right information from your resume and put it into the correct fields. You will save much time simply cutting and pasting information over from your resume to your profile, rather than fixing and deleting the results from the uploader.
2. **Limiting Your Connections:** Another mistake people make is listening to LinkedIn. LinkedIn tells you to only connect to people you know. But in order for LinkedIn to work, your network has to be big enough so that you are visible to those trying to find you, and you can see the folks you want to connect with. LinkedIn is not like Google. Your network has to be extensive enough (I think a total of 10+ million first, second and third-level connections) to be visible and work as a search engine.

Company Pages

LinkedIn gives you the ability to create a Company Page, and you automatically get the LinkedIn URL for your company page which is: LinkedIn.com/company/yourcompanyname. There is no need to customize it like you do your personal profile.

A LinkedIn Company Page gives you a free way to brand your business on LinkedIn that allows you to upload your logo, as well as add products and services. For each product or service, you can add photos, video, testimonials and recommendations from other LinkedIn members about them. You can highlight certain salespeople, and add special promotions just for your LinkedIn followers. You can even target specific industries with niche oriented banners.

LinkedIn also recently added "Company Updates" which allows followers of your company to see updates you write. As a Company Page administrator you will get to see statistics on your updates, such as impressions and activity percentages.

More on Measurement

There are two types of metrics you can measure on LinkedIn: *Qualitative Measurements* and *Quantitative Measurements.* Quantitative Measurements are usually associated with *numbers* and Qualitative with the *quality* of your engagement. Both are crucial to your success on LinkedIn.

Quantitative Measurements

Total Connections: You can find your total connections in a few places. Under the "Contacts" tab you will see "Network Statistics" and your total connections will be your first, second and third-level connections. You can get a quick glance at your number of connections and network size on your home page in a box called "Your LinkedIn Network."

New Connections: On your home page in "Your LinkedIn Network" click on the *New people* hyperlink and then click on first connections to see thumbnails of your connections. You want to keep an eye on these numbers to make sure they do not get stagnant. A little strategic growth every week can make all the difference to your success on LinkedIn.

LinkedIn Profile Views: Just above "Your LinkedIn Network" is "Who's Viewed Your Profile?" If you aren't getting at least ten views a week then chances are you are not getting as much business as you could out of LinkedIn.

LinkedIn Search Results: If you haven't done so yet, type the keyword or keyword phrase that best describes you into the "People" search field on the top right hand side of your profile. What page do you fall on? Again, it's good to get the baseline number now so you can see how much you improve later on!

Company Page Followers: If you have a Company Page on LinkedIn, then keep an eye on who is following you. Get that base line now.

Qualitative Measurements

Inbox Activity: Are you getting any inbox activity? Some of it will definitely be spammy in nature, but it's good to keep an eye on your inbox. Some people will want to genuinely reach and build a relationship with you. Are you getting any requests for business? This is probably one of the most important metrics to measure, and one of the main goals for being on LinkedIn.

LinkedIn Signal Keyword Mentions: Have you checked *LinkedIn Signal* to see how many of your keyword search terms (company name, your name, username, industry, product or service) are being mentioned? Once you set your metrics on *LinkedIn Signal*, all you have to do is click on your saved searches to see what new mentions you are getting.

Likes and Comments on Updates: Many people don't even realize you can monitor your own updates to see how often people liked or commented on them.

To find this, first Click on "Profile," and in the drop-down menu click on "View Profile." In your latest update, click on "See all Activity." Now you can see exactly what you have posted and how people have responded. If you are not getting many responses, consider adjusting what you post.

Group Growth and Interaction: If you have a group, you will want to keep an eye on your group growth and interaction. Check out how many members you have right now and make note of the changes going forward.

"Expert" Designation in Answers: Answers are one of my favorite tools for thought leader positioning on LinkedIn. One of the features is the "Best Answer" ranking given to the best answer by the person who posted the questions. Get enough best answers and you get listed as an expert in that category on the Answers homepage.

Recommendations: Are you getting recommendations? Are they thorough? Descriptive? From good people?

Participating in Groups

People should absolutely make use of the groups function on LinkedIn for three reasons. First of all, groups are a great way to connect with people outside of your network. Secondly, the information shared within groups might be very beneficial to your business. Thirdly, groups are a great way to position you as a thought leader expert.

To be honest, I have to tell you that I joined most groups just so that I could meet specific people. If you want to send a message to someone in LinkedIn who you are not directly connected to, you usually have to pay for an

"InMail," which LinkedIn values at about $10. However, you can message people who are not your direct connections if you share a group with them.

My own group Linkchat is associated with my *Tweet Chat* #LinkedInchat on Tuesday nights, and it's a great place where people can continue the conversation. There're a few more groups like that which I really pay attention to, because I know they've information that's pertinent to me.

Another great thought leadership builder is answering questions and contributing to discussions in groups. This takes a little bit more effort, because you really have to be diligent about monitoring and communicating within the group. But I've noticed that when I take the time to give thorough answers and contribute to the discussion, I almost always build new relationships that are good for my business.

LinkedIn Summary:

There's definitely a right way and a wrong way to use LinkedIn. When used properly, this robust, powerful platform can boost visibility and help you network with others more effectively. As Neil and Viveka have illustrated, taking the time to get to know the platform and experiment with its features can pay off—especially if your audience is mainly corporate executives or entrepreneurs.

The fourth platform on our list, YouTube, is more than a social media platform—it's also the second largest search engine behind Google. In fact, it was purchased in 2006 by Google. YouTube is the largest video-sharing website on the web, and offers businesses lots of opportunity to create and share content that gets them seen and heard by their audiences. The power of this visual platform lies in its extended reach, integration with

Google Search, and the value it provides for search engine optimization (SEO).

YOUTUBE

Statistics from YouTube.com[12]

- 60 hours of video are uploaded every minute, or one hour of video is uploaded to YouTube every second
- Over 4 billion videos are viewed a day
- Over 800 million unique users visit YouTube each month
- Over 3 billion hours of video are watched each month on YouTube
- More video is uploaded to YouTube in one month than the 3 major US networks created in 60 years
- 70% of YouTube traffic comes from outside the US
- YouTube is localized in 39 countries and across 54 languages
- In 2011, YouTube had more than 1 trillion views or almost 140 views for every person on Earth
- 500 years of YouTube video are watched every day on Facebook, and over 700 YouTube videos are shared on Twitter each minute
- 100 million people take a social action on YouTube (likes, shares, comments, etc) every week

What does this tell us? YouTube is the place to be for brand awareness and SEO. It is great for brand awareness because you can create how-to videos, promotional videos or video blogs on any topic, and if users view a similar video by your competitor, your video could show up on the same page in the "suggested" area.

For SEO, YouTube has a dual benefit. First, Google weights video highly in its organic search results. If someone types in the search phrase "how to paint a room," or "real estate Lexington Kentucky," videos optimized with keywords related to that search will tend to show up earlier in the search rankings.

Second, housing videos on a YouTube channel can be part of a "link-back" strategy for your website. Putting your website link on your channel as well as in your video descriptions creates multiple in-bound links to your website, which you can also expand by sharing your videos on other social channels.

It is also an effective client acquisition tool. People learn about you through your video content, then they click through to your website to learn more about you. You can build the "like, know and trust" factor very quickly using video.

When we talk to people about video, we always get a few who say, "That won't work for my business." For example: "I'm a CPA, how exciting is the tax code for video content?"

The truth is, there's not a business in the world that can't benefit from video. From entertaining videos to educational videos, product reviews and demonstrations, there's something for every audience. You just have to be creative. Come up with something fun, and people will share it.

For our CPA example, how about coming up with a funny rap song that explains the earned income tax credit? Or just simply sitting in front of a whiteboard and outlining the most common deductions people miss? Those could be entertaining and educational. Giving good information and putting a face and voice to your business can go a long way.

Here's another example. Imagine you sell blenders. How boring is that, right? Well, go to YouTube and type in "Will It Blend" and see just how entertaining blender sales can be! With over 190 million views, and over 400 thousand subscribers, Blendtec is one company that embraced all that YouTube had to offer and, according to Blentec's CEO Tom Dickson, Blentec sales shot up over 700 percent since launching their YouTube Channel.

We have used video strategies successfully for many of our clients, and they don't have to be expensive to produce. Some of the best shared content is self-produced. As long as people can get what you are saying, you don't have to spend a great deal of money.

For more examples of how video can work for your business, internationally-recognized video experts Lou Bortone and Pam Brossman shared their thoughts with us.

First, let's hear from Lou Bortone, an Online Branding Expert and Video Marketing Strategist with over 25 years experience as a marketing executive in the TV and entertainment industries.

> Small business is flocking to online video as a powerful marketing tool, and with good reason. Online video viewing is skyrocketing, with uber-video juggernaut YouTube leading the way. In fact, both YouTube and Cisco are making the bold prediction that soon 90% of all web traffic will be video. Video marketing is here to stay, so entrepreneurs must lead, follow or get out of the way!
>
> Online video is very effective because it creates a strong, personal connection, helping to increase the "know, like and trust" factor among your prospects and clients. Video can also help you enhance your online visibility and make you stand out in a crowded and competitive environment.
>
> Here are a few video marketing basics to get you on the right track:
>
> **Q:** What are some of the best ways to get started with online video?

A: How you approach video depends totally on your overall marketing strategy. Your video marketing plan should be based on your specific goals. With that in mind, some "must haves" include a video for your home page. This "welcome" video should be a short introduction to you and your services for anyone who visits your web site. This is your first impression video, so make it count.

You should also have a version of this video on your "About Me" page. However, even though this is your "about me" video, you should make it about them! In other words, focus on your viewer and let them know what you can do for them and why they should work with you. Keep it short and sweet, and always remember that your web visitor is thinking "WIIFM?" (What's in it for me?)

Q: What other types of videos are effective?

A: In addition to your "welcome" video, another excellent use of video is a "tips series" based on your particular area of expertise. Create a short series of one to two-minute videos and share your best tips for your niche. Your tips series can be posted on YouTube and on your own website. These videos are great for establishing trust and credibility with your target market.

Since these videos are meant to build credibility, don't make a pitch or an offer just yet. Remember to serve first, sell second. And because you're establishing a personal connection with your viewer, it's usually best to be on camera to deliver your tips. (As opposed to "screencast" videos like PowerPoint or screen captures where you're not on camera).

Q: What types of video content create the most engagement?

A: With so much video content available online, it's crucial that your videos are engaging and compelling. The best way to break through the clutter is to make sure your video is relevant to your target market. In short, don't be boring!

Whether or not you should be on camera or off camera again depends on your objectives. On camera videos are more personal and are usually best for touting your services or sharing your expertise. Off camera videos like screencasts or instructional videos can be very effective for teaching, product demos or sharing ideas.

Q: What is the best length for videos?

A: In today's attention-deficit society, the shorter your video, the better. Video should be no longer than it takes to effectively express your idea or message. As a general rule for promotional videos, two minutes or less is best. The exception is for instructional or demo videos, where you may need longer to teach or demonstrate your idea. So get right to the point and get on with it.

Q: What about equipment and editing?

A: When it comes to video, we tend to get hung up on technology. The truth is, all the equipment and technical know-how in the world is useless without a video marketing strategy. A low-tech video shot with a $50 webcam that features great content is far more effective than a fancy video that doesn't contain a compelling message. Focus on your content; the technology is less important.

Having said that, you can get started doing video with a simple webcam, or even by using the video feature on your iPhone or mobile device. As for editing, the same "keep it simple" rules apply. If you don't have your own editing program like iMovie, use YouTube's easy video editor to trim the front and back of your video and make it look spiffy!

Our second video marketing expert, Pam Brossman, is an international speaker, author, trainer and founder of the magazines, *SheExperts* and *Social Media Woman*. She expands on Lou's points regarding video types, equipment, timing and posting strategy:

> **Q:** What types of things can people do videos on?
>
> **A:** There are many ways that you can use videos in your business to connect, engage, attract, retain and convert customers, clients, leads and prospects. Below are just a few of the most popular ones:
>
> - **Video signatures:** Introduce yourself to prospective customers every time you send an email. You never know when someone may forward that email to a friend giving you the opportunity to connect with someone who may need your products and/or services
> - **Video newsletters:** Sharing engaging and informative content on a regular basis with your customers is a great way to provide value and continue your relationship with your current clients. Many people will share great newsletter information, giving you the opportunity to attract more clients.
> - **Video replies:** This is the most profitable video strategy that hardly anyone is using, but has the highest conversion outside of video sales funnels. It is the extra "WOW" factor that can seal the deal after a meeting, tender, proposal or new client acquisition. I have lost count of how many times we have secured high level customers and clients using this one strategy alone.
> - **Video training:** Developing training videos is a great list builder and positioning strategy for your business. People love to learn new things that they can implement to get a quick win. By providing video tutorials and using strategic video SEO to drive traffic to more

of your training, you not only grow your list, but position yourself as a leader in your marketplace.

Q: What types of video content creates the most engagement?

A: I have personally found that two types of videos get the most engagement:

- **Training videos**, where you teach something that your client or target market is really interested in learning [they always stay to the end]
- **Case study videos**, where you share a result or a story of how someone implemented a strategy or course of action and got the result that your target market is also interested in getting themselves

Q: Lighting, editing tips; do I need to have professional equipment?

A: Lighting and audio are probably the most important things you have to master when it comes to video.

Audio is definitely number one. If people cannot hear or understand you, then they will disengage immediately. They need to know what you're saying to learn, connect, interpret or enjoy the content.

Lighting is second. With everyone having HD quality video on their iPhones or on the latest flip cameras these days, there is no excuse for not having high quality video. However, that video is only as good as the lighting you provide. Don't shoot a video to get the gorgeous background of the ocean only to find that you are silhouetted and people cannot see you in the video. It is okay to shoot video outside, but sometimes it is better to take the video in the shade where there is even lighting. Sometimes it is even better to shoot when it is overcast than in direct sunlight.

Also, if you do not have lighting when inside,, try and shoot near a window on an angle where the sun lights up your eyes and your face is evenly lit.

Usually if you are doing webcam videos a well-lit room is fine—just make sure the audio quality is not hollow and that your background is tidy. If you have a spare room, you can set up your own studio and have the lights there ready for you to just pop in at any time and shoot a video. Lights can vary in price, but these days online suppliers offer some great packages if you look around.

Q: How long is best?

A: Length of video is a disputed question because each scenario is different. But here are our rules of thumb:

Shorter (two–three minutes):

- Sales video on your landing page with a call to action
- Promo videos for speakers and presenters
- Book trailers for authors: remember to leave them hanging so they MUST read your book
- Testimonials (60-90 seconds max)

Medium (up to five minutes):

- Case study testimonials
- Training

Longer (up to ten minutes):

- Product Launch videos: these can vary from 10-20 minutes and sometimes longer (if the training is good, people will stay to the end)
- Interview: Under 10 minutes max (If it goes longer do a Part 1 and Part 2; that way you can test it. If

people do not go and watch Part 2, then you know it was too long.)

Q: How often should you post a video?

A: Video is cumulative; the more you contribute, the bigger effect it will have on your results. We suggest a minimum two videos per month. I often recommend four per month – one per week or more is even better if you are a video blogger (you can shoot them all in one day and then distribute them every Friday or Monday on your blog, in your newsletter or on social media). The most important thing to note is repurposing that video. You have to maximize every video so that you are creating your own digital footprint all over the web. Make sure to include it:

- On your YouTube channel [video seo]
- On your blog
- On your social media channels
- On other video hosting sites

Also encourage other bloggers to feel free to use your video content as long as they attribute it to your website (for back-link and page rank benefits).

The more you have little pieces of video real estate out there working for you that are positioning you in your marketplace as a leader, the faster your business and bottom line will grow.

YouTube Summary:

In today's short-attention-span world, the power of video cannot be understated. As Lou and Pam have explained, just about any business can benefit from using YouTube, and you don't have to be a professional videographer to do so! It doesn't take a huge investment in equipment or knowledge, but it's important to start with a well-thought-out strategy. YouTube's power is in its integration with Google Search, its universal popularity and relative ease of use. We think it's a must-have component of both B-2-B and B-2-C social strategies.

Now that we've covered Facebook, Twitter, LinkedIn and YouTube, it's time to discuss our fifth platform, Google Plus. Although it's the newest of the five, we think this platform deserves serious consideration because it's so closely linked to Google search, which is still the most popular search engine. Google is constantly innovating and refining, so it's the force to watch as social media evolves. Let's take a closer look.

GOOGLE PLUS (also Google + or G+)

Statistics from OnlineMBA.com and TheSocialSkinny.com

- Google+ has had 90 million unique visitors
- More than 30% of those users are in the US
- Google+ users are 71% male
- The most common occupation of a Google+ user is an engineer
- 44% of Google+ users are "single"

- The Google+ button is served more than 5 billion times a day

What does this tell us? Although Google+ is a relatively new platform, its growth and integration in "all things Google" make it a powerful tool for business users, especially for SEO. The demographic is skewed more male (perhaps a bit more techy), but these are serious users who log in and share content regularly, with the lion's share being from the US.

Is Google+ right for your business? Well, the jury is still out. Some people swear by it—others aren't really sure yet. So we talked to three experts who have unique perspectives on the platform.

Chris Brogan, President of Human Business Works and owner of chrisbrogan.com, is first on our list. Chris is also the author of *Google+ for Business: How Google's Social Network Changes Everything*.

> **Q:** Early on in the platform's development, there was a lot of talk about jumping off of Facebook in favor of Google Plus. But should small businesses think in terms of Facebook vs G+? Should it really be either-or?
>
> **A:** I think small businesses have to ask whether their efforts on Facebook are netting more customers or more revenue. If not, then they might reconsider whether their presence on Facebook is adding value. That's something to research before just pulling out the rug.
>
> **Q:** Personal or Business Profile or both? In light of Google's search ranking system, is it essential to have both kinds of profiles on G+?
>
> **A:** For businesses, it's vital to have both types of profiles, and here's why. A personal profile is how one connects, plus it's also less restricted in actions to take than a busi-

ness profile. With both, you've got a chance to have overall brand "coverage" in the business profile, but be able to maneuver like a real live person with the personal page.

Q: In your experience, what kinds of businesses do well with G+? Can you point to some good small biz examples?

A: There are many small businesses still trying to wrap their minds around how to use G+ for their business, but Alure Home Improvement in New York is doing great as a small business on G+. What they're doing with it are things like highlighting the top things people do wrong when attempting a kitchen makeover or things that eat up too much money when you redo your bathroom—things like that. They have a services based business, but do a lot to showcase the value of choosing them as a home repair company. These kinds of posts end up being interesting information for people. They don't know who to trust when attempting one of these projects, but here's Alure talking about how to save money or the things people do wrong when they start down that path, and they're really trying to save you that mistake.

The Corcoran Group in New York is also one to watch. They're a real estate company, and what they show (instead of their homes), is interesting sites in New York that would make you think why New York is an interesting place to live—like restaurants or the shiny silver statue of Andy Warhol over by Union Square. They take these amazing photos that tell a story, and never once do they say, "Oh, and we have listings today." But should I want to buy a house in New York, I would go to the Corcoran Group.

G+ is a place where people connect on like interests. So if you are a photography person, there are now hundreds of thousands of photographers there. There are farmers there who share photos of their windmills and setups of

how they move cattle around and things like this. So the benefit is that there are lots of ways to share like interests.

Also, anything you share on G+ to the public domain immediately gets picked up in Google the search engine. All small businesses, whether or not they want to participate on the social web, are being talked about on the social web, and they're being searched on in search engines like Google.

Our second expert, Jesse Stay, is author of the book, *Google + for Dummies*, and elaborates on how and why businesses should be thinking about using the platform.

Q: Why do you feel Google + is a viable platform for small businesses?

A: Google+ is Google's way of socializing their search platform. If you currently have an SEO strategy, you need to be on Google+. With proper optimization, you can very easily rank your site higher than other sites that don't utilize Google+, just by having a Google+ profile. On Google, they are now ranking engagement over recency, and people over page rank. If you want to rank well on Google, you need a Google+ strategy. Search is the new SEO.

Q: Personal or Biz Profile or both?

A: As a small business, probably both. Your personal profile should be a means to reveal what's behind the covers for the Business Profile or brand. From a strategic standpoint, this allows you to attach authorship to articles and content on your website. At the same time you can link your profile picture and Google+ Profile back to your website and the content you create there. This also helps your content rank higher in Google search results.

Your business profile is where you represent your brand. Link it to your website. Link your website back to your Google+ profile. Add +1 badges and buttons so your content gains rank as more people +1 the content. Both of these strategies can lead to better search ranking on Google.

Q: In your experience, what kinds of businesses do well with G+? Can you point to some good small biz examples?

A: All businesses do well with Google+! If you want to rank well in search, you should be on Google+. You shouldn't be ranking your success on number of followers or the number of people commenting on your posts. Of course, that factors into search rankings, but the fact that you have a Google+ profile and your competitors don't should be enough of a factor towards a successful strategy. With the appropriate configuration, just having a profile on Google+ can immediately boost your search rankings on Google+.

As for good examples, I do really like the photographers that use Google+. Scott Jarvie is a good example. He uses it to share his talents with his audience. He holds contests where people can vote on their favorite pictures. I've seen other talent professions do well too–artists, musicians. Those with interesting stories to tell will do well. I really think every business has an interesting story to tell though, and if they figure out how to do it, and truly open the covers as they do so, they'll see success on Google+.

Elaine Lindsay, a Certified Social Media & Relationship Marketing Professional and Google+ evangelist had these things to add regarding the business benefits of G+:

> I feel G+ is a viable social platform for business for a number of reasons, but here are some important ones:
>
> Google is the #1 search engine on the Internet, YouTube is the second most popular search engine (and is owned by Google), and G+ is the social networking component of Google. Taking advantage of this triad and being on G+ with your personal and business page gives you more ways to get you and your brand out there. I believe G+ will eventually become the leader in the Google wheelhouse (*just my opinion*) which is yet another reason to have a G+ Business Page.
>
> G+ Pages are integrated directly into Google Search through a feature called "Direct Connect." When a user starts a search with the "+" sign, it will start bringing up Google+ Pages as they type. For example, typing "+TROOL Social" and clicking the #1 result will take you directly to the TROOL Social brand Page.
>
> Hangouts are another beneficial feature of G+. They're a great way to interact with your customers and potentials. Imagine having a live Q&A with up to ten people interested in your business/brand. They can see you and get a feel for your authenticity; it's a quick way to build trust.
>
> G+ can also be a valuable addition to your SEO toolkit for your website. Here's how: Add a G+ badge for both your personal profile and your company page to your website.
>
> The clean user interface of G+ makes it easy on the eyes and easy to read, with no distracting elements or features. There are games on G+, but you only see them if you play them in the personal area.

I also feel that businesses should have both a personal and business profile on G+ because they serve different functions. Your personal profile and those in your circles are where you begin to expand your connections. As you post more often and engage with others on G+, more people can find and follow your business page.

From your profile you can find circles to follow in a variety of places:

The shared Circles Database: This project was created by Chris Porter (http://goo.gl/PrcGo). #SharedCircles is a Google document with more than 50,000 names and over 400 circles shared.

Search: Search for a term you want inside G+ such as photographers or NASA. You can then circle some or all of the people in those circles. You can search for anything from within G+ and then further focus your search.

What kinds of businesses do well on G+? Here are three that I think show the divergent appeal of G+ business pages:

ChefHangout.com: A business page where you'll meet chefs from all over the planet as they lead cooking classes via G+. More than 25,900 people have ChefHangout's G+ page in circles.

Cortis Photographie: More than 5,000 people have Cortis Photographie (the business page of photographer Benjamin Cortis) in their circles, and over 50,000 people have Benjamin's personal profile in their circles.

Neighborhood Centers, Inc.: Neighborhood Centers, a community in Houston, Texas, is a non-profit organization that builds vibrant communities and keeps Houston a place of opportunity for all those working for a better life. More than 1,900 people have Neighborhood Centers, Inc. in circles.

There's no doubt in my mind that G+ is a good place for most businesses to be. In large part, I think it's due to Google's constant innovation. In fact, Vic Gundotra, Senior Vice-President of Social Business for Google, said that the company has been launching a new feature almost every day.

Google+ Summary:

Chris, Jesse and Elaine share some valuable insights into Google+, which seems to be holding its own among the top social networks. Google's continuous innovation and popularity as a search engine makes G+ integration attractive, and the business examples highlighted here can show you how others have been successful in using it. However, as with picking any platform, audience reach should be your highest priority.

5 Platforms = Plenty of Choices for Business Owners

As you can see from our interviews with the experts, there are many ways that business owners can benefit from incorporating one or more of the top social media platforms in their marketing mix.

The key to success is not to panic and try everything at once, but to look carefully at each platform and choose which ones make the most sense for your business. It can be hard not to succumb to the pressure of everyone jumping on the bandwagon—especially since everything that involves social happens quickly—but "slow and steady" wins the race.

Don't try to master multiple platforms at once... stand back and look at the big picture, and you'll be better able to choose wisely.

One More to Watch

One up-and-coming platform that we didn't discuss is Pinterest. Pinterest is a site for creating collections of photos and videos by "pinning" them to online boards. It has shown phenomenal growth in its early stages, but at this writing it's too early to tell how its use will shake out for business users. Right now there are some brands that are receiving lots of traffic from it via links to pictures on their websites.

Here again, however, the trick to success on this platform seems to be in the sharing and pinning non-commercial content. For instance, the online T-shirt retail company *Threadless* uses its Pinterest profile more for brand awareness than direct sales links to their online products. They share fun images of things people can make with recycled t-shirts.

If your product has visual appeal (especially for women, who dominate the platform) you may do very well to develop a profile on Pinterest, especially if you actively share and re-pin content from others, and comment and thank others for re-pinning your content. People aren't looking to be sold here. They are looking for fun, inspirational photos and videos to share.

For retail businesses interested in getting link-back, a good method is to add the Pinterest pin button to your website and/or online catalog pages. It works the same way as the Facebook "like" button and the Google "+1" buttons, making it easier for people who are browsing your site to share your visual content on their pin boards.

Time to take action:

Based upon your WHO and WHY, now write down which networks suit each goal you have. Then choose the network that will help you reach your biggest goal and focus on that one for the next 60 days.

Don't worry if it's Facebook and you have 10,000 Twitter followers, they'll wait for you to come back. The point is to focus your efforts in the right direction, and gain traction in one area before moving onto the next network.

Ok, you have the WHO, WHY and WHAT; now you need the HOW.

How are you going to implement your plan, and what are you going to talk about? Not knowing what to say week in and week out is one of the most common problems people face when using social media for marketing purposes.

You have a few choices for implementation. You can do it yourself; outsource it to either a virtual assistant or someone inside your office; or try a combination of the two.

Before we get into specifics on how you will implement, let's talk a little more about what engagement really means. The *Oxford Dictionary of Current English* defines the word "engage" in a variety of ways:

> "**engage v. (engages, engaging, engaged) 1** attract or involve someone's interest or attention. **2** (engage in/with) become involved in. **3** employ. **4** enter into a contract to do something. **5** enter into combat with. **6** (of a part of a machine or engine) move into position so as to begin to operate."

For our purposes, the first two definitions are all we need to worry about. First, we have to attract someone's attention. Secondly, we become involved in conversation with that person. How? By sharing helpful content with them.

By now, you've come up with your target market and we've talked lots about content strategy including using your blog as the hub of your social media efforts. You've also decided which one or two networks you will focus on for the next 60 days. Now let's think about your content strategy as a whole. What are you going to say and how are you going to say it? Also, how are you going to foster long term engagement with your growing community? Do you have the time and resources to handle your social strategy and engagement yourself, or will you outsource?

Doing it Yourself

There are different schools of thought on handling everything yourself or outsourcing all or part of your social strategy. However, we feel that if you can carve out the time, you should keep your social media marketing implementation in-house. It's easy to outsource tasks, but not so easy to outsource your voice, your company culture and message.

One of the biggest misconceptions of social media marketing is that it's free. Well, the tools are free, but your time (or an employee's time) is not. Do you have the time to implement your social media strategy correctly or train someone else on your staff to do it? If the answer is "no" then you may want to think about outsourcing (more on that later).

If you are going to do it yourself, we highly recommend in the beginning that you stick to one or two social media platforms in addition to your blog. Once you're on a roll, then you can add some others. Regardless of which network(s) you choose, a handy rule of thumb for not wasting time is using something we call the 3x15 Formula.

3x15 formula

Work on your networks
3 times per day
15 mins each

This schedule is in addition to writing your blog posts and posting original content to your social networks. That takes a little extra time. But 3x15 works well for moderating your social properties, posting and sharing articles, answering questions, responding to comments, tweeting and sharing content..

This is the fun part! Really get in there and get to know people. Create some real connections with your audience. You will find that the more you get involved, the more you enjoy interacting with people. Don't just post something and ignore it. Remember, this is supposed to be a two-way street.

A Few Tools for Keeping Track

Keeping track of the time is easy. There are free timers you can download to your computer or just use an egg timer, and set it for 15 minutes. Begin first thing in the morning. Check your blog for comments, Facebook page and so on. Don't get caught up in, "Oh how cute, Johnny and Susie had a baby..." social media can be a black hole if you let it suck you in. You have to focus!

Once the timer goes off, shut down the platform (don't have it running in the background) and get on with your other business.

At lunch repeat the same steps, and repeat again either before you leave the office for the day or before you go to bed. That's it!

As mentioned earlier, tools like *Hootsuite* and *Tweetdeck* allow you to manage and schedule your social interactions remotely. When you use your 15 minutes, you can schedule posts to drop at specific times, so it looks like you're at your computer at 10 am sending a tweet when in reality, you might be in a client meeting. You can schedule updates, re-tweets and @ replies for Twitter, page posts for Facebook and updates on LinkedIn. Strategically

utilizing these free tools will help you manage your success on social media easily.

Training Someone on Your Staff

Strapped for time and need to think about getting help? If you use someone in house, make sure social media duties don't just get tacked onto all their other responsibilities. They need the time to do it right. By now you see that it takes time, effort and energy to be effective on social media. Don't expect an already overwhelmed employee to be able to create a successful community if they can't focus on doing it. If you want to do it right, you will need to have the time to do it or make the time for someone else to do it.

Also, do not hire or use a college intern just because they are young and "on Twitter." It takes years to develop a marketing brain. Being well-schooled in social media best practices is a good thing, but find someone who wants to become an expert in your brand; someone who is a natural at creating relationships. They understand that not everything is a revenue event, but everything is a relationship event.

Stay in the Loop

Keep in mind that it's important for you to be involved in at least the conversational part of a social media campaign. For instance, someone in your organization should know when people comment on a post or re-tweet your information, so they can follow up and extend the conversation. However, you should know this as well. You may not have actually written the post, but it would be helpful to know that a client (or colleague) retweeted your blog or commented on one of your Facebook posts yesterday.

Also, it's important for you to understand the nuances of social media and how best to create a strategy. Your team should keep you up to date about who they think are "super fans" or "super followers" so you can reach out to them personally. You also need a social media plan in place to deal with positive and (unfortunately) negative comments (more on that later in this chapter). Consider having a written social media policy for your internal employees that governs online communications.

Outsourcing

If you don't have someone on your internal business team you can use, there are resources for finding social media virtual assistants to help you. A virtual assistant (VA) is someone who works remotely and manages your social media campaigns. It is a great way to get the help you need without incurring the costs of hiring an employee, since most VAs work as 1099 independent contractors. However, there are lots of "so-called" social media virtual assistants out there. You want to make sure that the service you hire actually knows what they're doing and has a track record.

One of the companies that we have used to supplement our client's online interactions is BizMSolutions, an agency of trained social media VAs who mainly cater to small business. Janice Clark is the owner as well as a Certified Social Media Consultant, and outlines below some of the do's and don'ts of hiring a social media VA.

Q: What kind of tasks can a VA help with?

A: A good VA can assist with almost every step in your social media campaign. Just a few of the most common tasks include:

- Researching potential partnerships, clients, etc., and adding those strategic connections on each of your sites
- Researching quality information to post on your behalf
- Creating tweets/posts from your current content
- Scheduling posts in advance on your accounts

- Syndicating your content out to a variety of networking sites to provide you with maximum visibility
- Setting up your shopping cart and mailing list software
- Creating online profiles for your social networking sites that are designed to showcase your expertise and the benefits of working with you

Q: What tips can you give small business owners for finding "qualified" social media VAs to help with outsourcing social media tasks?

A: First, look for someone who is actually doing these tasks for themselves. Knowing how to tweet and post is entirely different from understanding how to create a working strategy and maintain the consistency it takes to get results.

If a VA can't get connections, partnerships and referrals for themselves via their networking sites, then they can't do it for you. If they don't create and syndicate their own content, they won't understand the challenges you face either.

Secondly, their website needs to be professional and the VA needs to be able to intelligently offer recommendations for your site and your strategy, and should be able to fluently discuss a variety of jobs they have held in the past. They may not be able to give you specifics of exactly what they did, but they should be able to offer you examples of the results they achieved for their clients.

Q: What are some key pitfalls to avoid?

A: A social media VA might not be the best fit if they:

- Can't discuss past results they've achieved
- Haven't successfully used social media for their own business

- Don't have a strong following online (It's ok if they don't have 20,000 followers, but if they only have 30, then you know there's a problem)
- Don't have a blog that is updated regularly with good content
- Only use one or two social networking sites for themselves
- Can't tell you what they're doing to stay on top of the latest social media trends
- Thinks social media marketing is the only type of marketing you need
- Promises great results quickly
- Can't intelligently discuss a strong content syndication strategy
- You know more than they do about social media.

It's too easy to get into trouble online if the VA isn't aware of the rules and etiquette surrounding each networking site. Ultimately, if you have to explain individual tasks to them and feed them information about what to do next, then they aren't going to be an asset and you aren't going to be satisfied.

Q: Is there a range people can expect to pay for good social media help (depending on the level of service)?

A: Between $35–$120 per hour is normal. Very often you can find an excellent basic social media assistant for $35–$55 per hour. If they charge less than $35 they probably aren't very experienced and could end up costing you a lot more in the long run. Higher priced VAs should be able to help you create and implement a full social media marketing and content marketing strategy.

Janice brings up some very important points to consider when hiring a VA, but the bottom line is… be careful. Although there can be a lot of pressure to jump into social quickly and farm out the day-to-day tasks that take up so much time, we recommend being very cautious when outsourcing these tasks. Your daily interaction on social platforms forms the basis of your brand's social credibility, and handing that off to someone without monitoring what they're doing (or knowing what to look out for) is a recipe for disaster.

Outsourcing Content Creation

As we've mentioned, one of the most difficult parts of social media marketing is the content creation, and this is another area where you might want to consider outsourcing. You may be spending hours upon hours trying to come up with something to say on your blog, writing the posts, searching for royalty-free images and writing witty, short updates for your networks. It can all be overwhelming.

There are lots of online sources for freelance writers to help with your content. Just be sure they're professional marketers, not generic article writers. Also, be sure they understand your goals and your industry. You want your updates to be written in such a way that they encourage people to comment and repost to their networks. When hiring a freelance writer to produce your content, you should expect to pay $25-$100 per blog post for professional quality. There are tons of low-level writers out there. Don't be tempted to hire them just because they're cheap. Poor quality writing hurts your credibility in the marketplace.

If you're fighting the "blank page syndrome" and have a limited budget, one low-cost article-writing service we recommend is *Textbroker.com.* If you're in the early stages of blogging, you can use Textbroker to get blog posts written on generic topics for as little as 12 cents a word. You'll want to pay close attention to the finished articles and edit them, but this can help get you started.

Planning Your Engagement Strategy

Once you have an idea of the resources you'll need for writing content and handling social media activities, you'll need to plan your social media content strategy carefully. This is a very important step. What will you say and how will you say it? You might want to bookmark the following sections, because you will need to refer to these sections before you write a word of content.

Listen First

We always recommend that before you start writing, use your social channels for listening in on certain keywords relating to your business, your company or your competitors. Use *Search.Twitter.com*, *Google Alerts*, or the *Facebook Search* function to listen in on what is being said about you, and your product or service.

There are some paid programs out there (in a variety of price ranges) that can help you with this as well. Depending on your budget, you might explore several of these to see what services would best suit your business. Some popular paid programs include small-business tools like *SproutSocial* and *RavenTools*, and more expensive enterprise-class tools such as *Radian6* and *Scoutlabs*.

The important thing to remember is that you need to develop a baseline. Find out what's currently being said about you and your brand, and where you currently stand in the social space. Also do the same for your competition. This is a great way to see where you stack up against your competition in the social space.

Finding out what, if anything, people are saying can also reveal some fences you may need to mend before beginning a social media campaign. Make sure you blend that into your social media strategy. Begin by addressing those issues, so you don't jump into a swarm of bad publicity.

Once you've listened thoroughly, then you are ready to talk intelligently to your audience. This can be the most paralyzing step for people. What do I say? What if I say the wrong thing? Don't sweat this too much. We're going to outline some things to watch out for.

What Not to Post

There are many great things you can come up with to find material for your posts. We've outlined sources for you (Google trends, Google reader, other people's blogs, your own customer research, etc.), but it is also important to discuss what you shouldn't post. There have been some pretty high profile stories about major brands who have posted the wrong thing at the wrong time:

High Profile Social Media Mistakes

- Kenneth Cole sent out a tweet in very poor taste during the uprising in Egypt that got his fashion house brand boycotted by many people[13].
- Kentucky Fried Chicken Thailand made a misstep when they posted on their Facebook page: "Let's hurry home and follow the earthquake news. And don't forget to order your favorite KFC menu.[14]"
- Motrin had a promotional video in which a woman said that wearing a baby sling is a great way to bond with her child, but that it can also cause the mother great pain. This video was controversial with its target market, and it quickly went viral:

  > Not so great when the feedback included mothers vehemently protesting it. There were blog posts, tweets, Facebook updates, and more about the offending campaign[15].

These are just a few of the many examples where brands did not think their posts or campaigns through. Sage advice: take a moment in private before posting in public. Keep in mind that whether you do your own posting our you have an administrator do it for you, public pages are just that—public.

Other types of posts to avoid would be in keeping with things your parents probably told you: "If you can't say anything nice, don't say anything," (this applies to your competition) and "Don't discuss politics or religion" (unless your brand caters to the political or religious, it's best to steer clear). This includes re-tweets or shares of peoples' posts. A re-tweet or share can be interpreted as an implied endorsement of that content; something to think about when you train your employees or before you hit the RT or share button.

So, what do you say and when? With our clients, we map out the content strategy using a great tool called a content calendar.

Using a Content Calendar

You've undoubtedly spent a lot of time organizing your business procedures, and you'll need to do the same for your content. Whether you're a spreadsheet kind of person or you would rather work from a handwritten to-do list, having a month-at-a-glance tool for organizing your social content is essential. You can create one from scratch using WORD or Excel, or even populate your Google or Outlook Calendar with content for posting. We are sharing the one we use as a complement to this book, and it can be downloaded at

http://solvingthesocialmediapuzzle.com/calendar/.

No matter what style calendar you choose, it helps to brainstorm your editorial in "sets" that make it easier to segment tasks. Here are some tools we use to populate content calendars:

- **Come up with themes for each week of the month.** A theme could be a sale, a speaking engagement, seasonal tips, recent news, or local business spotlights. Using themes for every week of content can help you categorize your updates. Some like to do this quarterly, some monthly or weekly. Do whatever works for you, as long as you do it.

- **Keywords are another tool you can use for theming.** Have your keyword bucket handy when brainstorming your topics. Think about the questions you heard in your listening phase—what people are asking about—and jot them down.
- **Keep in mind your big events of the year, and plug those into your calendar as well.** Do you have seasonal sales planned for your brick-and-mortar or online retail business? Are there industry events you will be attending? Webinars you will be conducting? Plot them in your calendar to make it easy to plan blog and/or social post topics around them strategically.
- **Start with sketching out your blog titles.** Our social media marketing calendar has the days of the week listed down the left side, and the platforms used across the top, starting with "Blog." Write your blog title first, then go across each platform box and write in some content that will go along with each post (or just a keyword to remind you). Keep going until they are filled, and you'll know exactly what you're supposed to be talking about each day.

Remember, an ongoing listening regimen will help you get a sense of what's being discussed so you can plan appropriate content, react to good (or bad) news, and keep an eye on what your customers are looking for.

What To Do if Feedback is Negative

One of the most common reasons businesses avoid social media is fear that someone will post negative things about them or their brand. As we covered in Step Four, you can be assured that the conversation is going on about your brand, whether or not you are present. Wouldn't it be better to be able to redirect negative comments and potentially turn detractors into brand advocates?

We know from our own experiences that generating and achieving customer loyalty can be as simple as responding when your customer is unhappy. Many times your clients just want to know that you heard them and that you acknowledge there may be a problem and will try and fix it. However, sometimes that's not enough. Rather than being reactionary or scrambling for an answer, it's best to have a protocol in place for dealing with negative situations.

Develop an Action Plan

For larger brands, it's imperative to decide these strategies ahead of time. When we're working with clients, we always ask the question: "What are you going to do if people respond to your postings either positively or negatively?" For example, when having an initial "onboarding" meeting with one of her clients, a major laundry detergent brand, Kathryn asked what would happen if someone posted that their laundry detergent burned a hole in their clothes—or worse, they accuse the brand of causing personal injury. That was something the company hadn't considered. She worked with the client to put in place a plan that took into account the innocuous complaint or question (e.g., The coupons won't print; What kinds of clothes can I use this on? etc.), all the way to the worst case—someone was injured.

First, she conducted a listening campaign for the first month. This included more closely monitoring the social channels to determine what, if any, consistent complaints or questions arose.

Next, she compiled a document that included set responses to common questions and complaints. Both Twitter and Facebook responses were drafted—approximately 20-30 for each. That way the client's legal department could review and approve them, but customers would get a response more quickly and the responses did not look "canned." She also performed the same exercise for other types of posts, including compliments. This way all communications were covered and the client was able to engage more quickly. Below are some generic examples:

> Complaint: We're sorry that you're having trouble, [FAN NAME]. Please contact customer service at [800# or email] so that we can take care of this for you ASAP.
>
> Compliment: Thank you [FAN NAME]. It always makes us feel good if we can help make life a little easier for our friends.

Note: No matter which networks you choose to work with, use the person's name if possible when responding. Sometimes it takes a few more seconds to track down their real name, but it makes people feel acknowledged.

Kathryn's plan also included a list of which types of comments and questions needed to be routed to different departments. For example, if someone said that their product caused injury, those comments would be routed to the legal department for review and response.

In the case of Facebook, brands could not message fans directly when Kathryn first drafted the plan, so she set up a special "Facebook moderation" email address that was routed to customer service. This email address was to be posted on the reply to a comment if the moderator felt that it warranted further brand involvement.

There are several online tools that help with customer service (particularly with Facebook). Once such tool is *Parature*, a Facebook client services paid tool that uses keywords to route consumer questions and complaints to individuals within an organization. Using this tool allowed Kathryn's client to keep a better handle on the types of comments and to also be sure that they were routed to the correct person or department more quickly.

Lastly, the team decided specifically who would be responsible for responding to issues. It was clear that if they did not have a plan in place, or someone experienced to handle it, things could go bad quickly; so they drafted a social media policy for distribution to all departments.

There is little doubt that someone will eventually post negative comments to you or your brand, but being prepared is the key. If your brand is under attack, your first reaction may be to defend it. For instance, a senior executive once replied to a Facebook post from his personal profile, blaming the customer for an issue without realizing that he was posting as himself. Another team responded to a negative comment on a blog post by calling the poster an "idiot and a liar.[16]" Mistakes such as these just make a bad situation worse, but can easily be avoided if a plan is in place. Make sure you have one!

Time to take action:

Think about how much time you have available each day and decide the smartest way to use your time.

Will you write and post everything yourself? Will you outsource everything? Or will you outsource only the content creation (blog posts and social media updates) and concentrate on the fun part of interacting using the 3x15 method?

On this page, write down four themes you can use over the next month:

CONTENT THEMES

THEME 1:

THEME 2:

THEME 3:

THEME 4:

Get started on your "Negative Comment Plan" by jotting down the possible negative comments people could make about your brand, product or service (be honest with yourself here). Ask your customer service team or other customer-facing employees to submit ideas as well.

Step Six: Measuring Results

By now you should have most of the pieces of the puzzle in place. You know who you're targeting, where they reside online, what platforms and content you will use—you've even got your calendar all plotted out. That was easy, right?

But how do you measure your results? What metrics will you use? With the help of our experts, we covered some of the metrics for specific platforms in Step Four, but now it's time to quantify your goals.

For example, if your goal is brand awareness, you might say you want to increase your fan base of targeted fans by ten percent in 60 days. If your goal is increased blog traffic, you can say you want to reach 3,000 readers in the next 90 days.

The point is, you must track your results somehow. How will you know if your time is being well spent if you don't track your outcome? Also, remember the **PETT** acronym for plan execute, track and tweak? Tracking your progress will allow you to more quickly tweak your social media campaigns to make them more effective.

We talked about some of the free tools available that help you track progress, such as *Google Analytics, Google Alerts, Social Mention, Search.Twitter.com* and Facebook and YouTube *Insights. Hootsuite*, the social media scheduling platform we mentioned earlier also gives some metrics to help you track your progress.

We also mentioned some of the paid tools like *SproutSocial*, that help measure your reach on Facebook and Twitter (other popular paid tools are listed in the Resources section of this book).

However, many business owners are confused about exactly how to measure social effectiveness. How do you really know what's working? Which numbers should you be tracking?

We asked a digital marketing expert, Paul Mosenson, some questions that business owners ask regarding what and how to measure social initiatives. Paul is founder of the virtual marketing agency NuSpark Marketing and author of the e-book, *A Practical Guide to Lead Generation and Social Media.*

> **Q:** For businesses just getting started in social media, what is the best way to measure how well they're doing?
>
> **A:** This is a question that comes up a lot; the issue is how you define and identify "what's working?" With social media, you have to be clear with your objectives up front and determine benchmarks for measurement. Typically there are three categories of social media objectives:
>
> 1. **Build Reach:** Website traffic, Site Conversions, Social Connections
> 2. **Increase Customer Service:** Customer Satisfaction, Community Building
> 3. **Enhance Branding:** Awareness, Thought Leadership, Innovation
>
> For a business just getting started, the first goal of any social media plan is user engagement. Every post, tweet and update is designed to elicit a response from an interested user, whether that response is an actual comment, share, favorite, +1, re-tweet, or a Like. If your social media posts are interesting, compelling, targeted and written properly, those posts are more likely to generate an engaged audience willing to be part of the conversation. Many social media tools and platforms exist that can easily measure engagement.

Engagement leads to the most important measure of social media; revenue. As a business, your goal is to generate revenue no matter what channel or media tactic you use. Social media is not easily tied into revenue unless you're using the platform to promote a specific offer and can track the conversions. Therefore you have to consider how social media usage affects your overall website traffic (using a tool like *Google Analytics*), traffic from social media events (like blogs), engagement goals (time on site, pages per visit), and conversion goals (purchase, lead, newsletter, contact).

In summary, if your activity is attracting quality prospects, and you're engaging them with quality content and conversation, you're off to a good start. Over time, keep an eye on your analytics and study website visitor growth and conversion rates.

Q: Are there some tools you recommend for measuring success for various platforms?

A: Well, there seem to be hundreds of social media tools out there; choosing the right platform is a matter of taste, features, usability, and cost. Social media measurement tools that track engagement generally fall into two categories:

1. **Multi-platform:** These dashboards allow you to post and track multiple social media channels. Some of the more popular tools are *Hootsuite, SproutSocial, Awareness Social Marketing Hub, Spredfast,* and *Social Report.*
2. **Single platform:** These are either measurement tools that are included within the platform, like *Facebook Insights* and *YouTube Analytics*, or third-party tools that use the platform API, such as *Twitalyzer* for Twitter. Google promises some measuring tools for Google+, but at this writing they are not available yet

in the platform itself; however, the effect of +1s are now being tracked via *Google Analytics.*

Q: Should every business owner already be using Google Analytics for their website? How can that tie into social?

A: *Google Analytics* is the standard for small business, because it's free, although paid web analytics tools such as *Woopra* and *Clicky* also have some unique features. The goal of any marketing initiative is to "fill the funnel," that is, to have a number of prospects journeying through a marketing process that begins with brand awareness and ends with purchase of your product or service (also called conversion). Fortunately, *Google Analytics* has recently expanded its social media measurement offering to help us track the effect that social media channels have on conversions, whether they are last-click conversions or assisted conversions (those that are attributed to other channels like organic search).

A simple diagram of such a funnel is shown on the next page, where the new Google Analytics Social Media Reports listed on the right of the diagram correspond to the stages of the conversion funnel on the left.

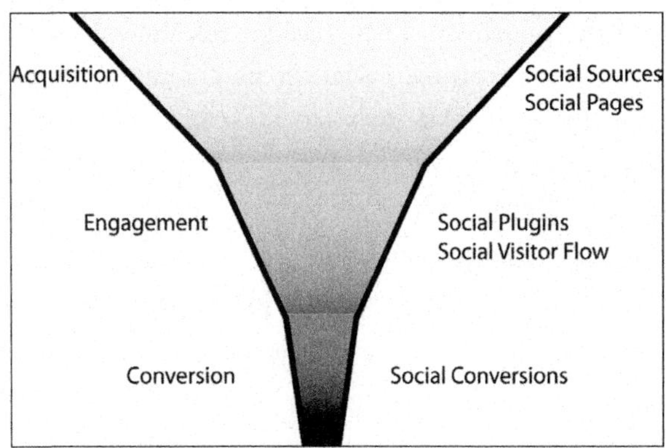

Another way to measure social media engagement with Google Analytics is to create advanced segments. Advanced segments are customized audiences over and above Google's default segments. By default, Google treats social media channels as referral sites. Therefore advanced segments separate social media referral sites from other referral sites. So by creating advanced segments in Google Analytics, you can get better data to help you discover how social media users behave on your website.

Q: When clients ask you about the ROI of social, what do you tell them?

A: It's a similar question to when people used to ask me about the value of public relations. You really can't measure ROI from a direct sense, because social media is not about hard-sell promotional messages. However, social media is probably the most influential medium, because audiences rely on their peers and connections for advice and recommendations.

Many bloggers and thought leaders try to ascertain social media ROI by utilizing sophisticated formulas. It's my opinion that those bloggers don't get it. It's vital to understand the medium; building message credibility, offering good, interesting content, and contributing to conversation. Once established as a trustworthy thought leader, the leads you get will be qualified, and more likely to purchase.

Going back to analytics, if you see your overall site traffic increasing over time, and you show an increase in conversions and conversion rate across all channels, then social media is having an impact.

What About Measuring Advertising?

Tracking the effectiveness of your posts, updates and tweets may not be as simple as an ROI calculation, but performance of

Pay-per-click (PPC) and Cost-per-impression (CPI) ads, such as those used by Facebook and LinkedIn, can and should be tracked closely to measure their effectiveness in driving traffic. Ads can be an important factor in driving new traffic to your Facebook or LinkedIn profiles, and it's worth experimenting with them to see what works.

We asked, Chris Treadaway, co-author of the book, *Facebook Marketing in an Hour a Day*, for tips on how to use social media ads (particularly Facebook advertising) effectively.

Q: In your experience with measuring social media effectiveness, how important do you think ads are in the grand scheme of things?

A: They're important really in two different ways. The primary reason to invest in ads is to accentuate your earned media efforts. A small percentage of businesses can get away with no advertising, usually because their value proposition is very unique or because their brand is known because they've spent millions if not billions of dollars on advertising over the years. But a vast majority of us are trying to get attention for what we're doing, and it is pretty easy and cost-effective to throw money at the problem. It works.

The other reason to advertise is to get a larger number of eyeballs on a new marketing initiative. It's good for relatively inexpensive testing of ideas, concepts, businesses, and product marketing plans.

Q: Can you give us some examples of the kinds of data that businesses should be trying to mine from social—and how it can benefit them?

A: We are very early in social data mining, but it's an area with a ton of promise. If you think back to product registration cards that we used to get as recently as about a decade ago – those were slipped into product packaging to help marketers better understand who their customers are. Now you can get all that data and more from mining social media properly. In addition, you can get that information on your competitors. So the benefit is really another level of understanding about customers and your competitive environment, which is something marketers always want.

Q: In your experience with Facebook ads, is there an optimum sweet spot for length of campaign—number of impressions?

A: The key is to both give your customers enough impressions for them to notice your offering, for them to have enough time to subconsciously think about it, and for them to ultimately act upon the AD. Unfortunately, that doesn't really happen with a single impression per user. Really the optimum level depends on AD budget, targeting criteria, and AD creative as well. We typically try to run no less than 10 impressions per AD permutation, per user in the target market before drawing any conclusions.

Q: What top mistakes do you see smaller business make in terms of measuring (or not measuring) results?

A: The small business community is getting smarter about demanding results, which is good. But the trend I see now is that people take that too far – an over-reliance on measurement. If you're going to be a great marketer, I think you have to understand that you can't measure everything. You're going to get some invisible benefit from all your marketing activities – people will remember your product or business even if they don't click an AD. The best marketers I know use measurement as a tool, but don't obsess over it.

Q: What's your opinion on the importance of testing and tweaking?

A: Testing and tweaking are critical, but you have to be able to isolate outcomes to know that changes are warranted and that you've improved. The first things you do rarely ever work in just about anything you're doing for the first time. This is no different.

Whether you're measuring social advertising that Chris Treadaway talks about or traffic to your website via Google Analytics or the other measurement tools that Paul Mosenson mentioned, keep this important caveat in mind:

Sometimes social media is working like crazy even when you can't directly track the results!

This is where many people give up and move on... when they just don't see any immediate visible results. But that's like a farmer planting an apple seed, and coming back a week later saying "Hmmm, no apples. It must not be working." With social media, you need to take a long-term view, realizing that your efforts are having an effect even if you don't see immediate conversions.

This is exactly why you need a solid plan; so you don't have to spend a ton of time on any one aspect of social media marketing. The farmer doesn't spend every minute of his day tending to a single apple tree, but he does provide consistent nurturing.

The important thing is not to get caught up in "analysis paralysis" with measurement, but to move forward with your plan and tweak it as you go. Use measurement as an overall guide to help you plan and execute your strategy.

Step Seven: Putting it All Together

The last, most important step in our seven-step process is to incorporate your newly-minted social media strategy with your traditional marketing efforts. Why is this so important? Because everything you do outside of social media, such as your website, email marketing, public relations and print advertising needs to dovetail with your social efforts to be truly effective. Don't worry, it's not as hard as you think—but it does require a well thought out plan.

First, take the time to put the exercises we've discussed in this book into a living, breathing, document that you can use to plan, execute, track and tweak your social strategy:

- Persona creation and target market
- Blogging content
- Choosing objectives
- Choosing the social media channel(s)
- Management decisions and tools
- Measurement tools and metrics

It doesn't matter what kind of document (WORD, Google Docs, Excel, etc.), as long as it's easy for you to make changes.

Second, once you have this document in place and you've decided which platforms you'll be using, make sure to include links to those platforms in the following critical areas:

- **Website:** Include the social sharing badges or boxes for the platforms you'll be using in an easy-to-spot place on your website. We recommend placing them in an area where people are most likely to see them, rather than burying them at the bottom of your page. Think "above the fold," such as near your navigation header or at the left or right of your pages. Each platform has its own HTML code for these badges which you can configure. Then it's a matter of either you or your web designer cutting and pasting that code in the appropriate place in the HTML of your website.
- **Email:** Incorporate all of your social platform links in your basic email signature. This is an easy way for people you connect with on a daily basis to follow you on your various platforms. Got a newsletter that you send out regularly? Many of the well-known email clients, such as Constant Contact® or MailChimp, have social sharing and/or social connect buttons you can enable on those campaigns. Check with your email provider to see what's available and how you can incorporate them in your email template.
- **PR:** Send out periodic press releases? Be sure to include links to your social platforms on every release, so that both news agencies and other readers know where to find you on social channels. Make use of QR (quick response) codes that people can scan with their mobile devices to send them to your social links. These work particularly well at events or in print.
- **Print:** Include social display buttons and/or links in all your print advertising (business cards, letterhead, direct

mailings, billboards, publication ads, posters, etc.). Even if these cannot be working links, make sure people can easily see all the places they can connect with you. As with PR, you can use scannable QR codes on print material. They are a great way to let people find your social channels directly from their mobile phones. Most smart phones have QR code reader applications.

Third, once all your traditional marketing pieces have social sharing and/or follow integration, take a look at your traditional lead generation activities, such as article publication, free reports, events, radio or television. Hopefully, you have these activities planned out in advance—so go back to your social media editorial calendar and plug those things in as early as you can.

For example, if you have an event planned, such as a booth at a convention, you may want to include some video taken at the event as blog posts and schedule updates in other platforms. Plan that out in advance. Another example would be writing a white paper or special report. Don't just post it on your website—be sure to plan a launch strategy in your social calendar before, during and after you publish the document to give your report longer shelf life.

In short, take a closer look at all your traditional avenues and look for ways to weave them into your social calendar. This takes a bit of thought, because you don't want to be too promotional in your social content. However, you'll soon become adept at "thinking out of the box" when it comes to melding your traditional and social efforts.

So there you have it: a complete, 7-Step Social Media Marketing Planning Guide that lets you build your business and still have time for a life.

Don't forget... once you've decided on your social media plan, we recommend that you stick to it for at least 60 days, mastering one network at a time until you have achieved your business objectives. Remember, you don't have to be everywhere if you don't have the time and resources. Choose at least one network and strategy and go for it!

Let's go over everything one more time quickly:

7 Simple Steps:

- **Identify Your Market:** Identify your audience by creating personas and developing a listening campaign to find out what people are saying about you—and what they're looking for as it relates to your brand.
- **Set Clear Objectives:** Write down clear, measurable objectives for what you want to get out of social media marketing, and figure out your internal and external resources for getting things done.
- **Plan Your Blog Content:** The hub of successful social media marketing is content. Without it, your social wheel collapses. Organizing a blog is the easiest way to provide regular, deep content that feeds your social communications. A well-executed blog also positions you as a thought leader in your industry, and keeps your brand higher in search engines.
- **Choose Your Social Platforms:** Once your audience and objectives are clear and your content source is planned, you can then select the appropriate channels and develop an overall content plan. Work on mastering one platform at a time.
- **Engage Wisely:** Decide whether or not you will outsource all or parts of your content plan, and develop engagement policies where appropriate. Incorporate a listening campaign to establish a baseline for moving forward with content development, and use an editorial calendar to flesh out your content offerings. Keep it flexible.

- **Track and Measure:** Create social ads where appropriate to drive traffic to your content, and measure the results of every initiative. Use the many tools available for visualizing where you are in relation to your overall goals. Keep track of page visits, re-tweets, shares, likes and conversations as indicators of how well your content is working.
- **Put it All Together:** Integrate your social media marketing strategy with your traditional marketing efforts. Make sure that your customers and prospects can find you on social channels via ALL of your marketing initiatives by integrating social sharing and following options into your website, lead generating materials, PR, email and print advertising. Make it a habit to think in terms of social when planning any marketing activities so you can easily incorporate them into your content calendar.

Planning a good social media marketing strategy really begins and ends with your audience. Starting with identifying the people you want to reach and really honing in on their needs and desires will help you piece together the other parts of the puzzle—right down to incorporating your social plan with other marketing initiatives.

Remember that social media is first and foremost a form of communication—a way to build relationships. Keep that in mind, and always strive to provide value, rather than blasting sales messages. It can help to think of our acronym **PETT** (Plan, Execute, Track and Tweak) when planning each segment of your social media marketing. Using the simple steps we've outlined in this book will help you master social communication and build the right kind of relationships—those that continue to be fruitful for both you AND your customers for years to come.

Kathryn Rose

Kathryn Rose is an award-winning author, speaker, social media strategist and trainer with clients ranging from multi-million-dollar corporations to small business owners and entrepreneurs. She has a twenty-plus-year career in sales and marketing and has created successful communities for her clients totaling over two million fans, followers and connections.

Prior to her career in social media marketing, Kathryn was a top Wall Street sales executive, responsible for over $100 million in sales per year. She used her collaboration skills to partner with sales people from other companies to form a lucrative referral network. A sought-after social media and relationship marketing speaker and trainer, Kathryn is also the CEO of the Social Buzz Club, the world's first online marketing collaboration network.

She is the author of six books on social media marketing: *The Step by Step Guides to: Twitter, Facebook, SEO/Video Marketing and Linkedin for Business* and *The Parents' and Teens Guides to Facebook* as well as co-author of the book *Solving the Social Media Puzzle: 7 Simple Steps to Planning a social media Marketing Strategy for Your Business* and the upcoming *Return on Relationship: Relationships ARE the new currency — honor them, invest in them, and start measuring your ROR!*

Kathryn is a sought-after keynote speaker on topics ranging from marketing and sales to social media and online marketing. Her speaking credits include: Ladies Who Launch Global Conference, Small Business Success Summit, Internet Week and Women Entrepreneurs Rock the World, among others.

Kathryn has been featured in *Woman's Day*, *Fox Business News* and *genConnect*. She lives in the Boston area with her husband and two children.

Connect with Kathryn:

Website: www.KatRoseConsulting.com
www.SocialBuzzClub.com
Email: Katrose1@gmail.com
Facebook: www.facebook.com/katrose
Twitter: www.twitter.com/katKrose (@katKrose)
Linkedin: www.linkedin.com/in/katKrose
Google +: www.plus.ly/KatRose
Pinterest: www.pinterest.com/katKrose
Youtube: www.youtube.com/socialmediapuzzle

Apryl Parcher

As an award-winning writer, copywriter and journalist with over 25 years of business experience, Apryl is a marketing content expert. She has written highly targeted marketing copy for organizations across the United States and Europe, from small businesses to Fortune 1,000 companies, and has owned and operated several small businesses in both retail and service sectors. Through her consulting and marketing business, Parcher Marketing Associates, she provides lead generating web and print material for both B-2-B and B-2-C clients

In addition to providing lead generating content for her clients, Apryl is Certified Social Media Consultant. She continues to study with industry leaders such as Mari Smith, and helps independent professionals and business owners assimilate a focused social strategy into their marketing plans. She also serves as Social Media Content Director at NuSpark Marketing, a virtual marketing agency in Philadelphia that offers broad-based content marketing solutions for business.

Apryl is co-author of the book *Solving the social media Puzzle: 7 Simple Steps to Planning a Social Media Marketing Strategy for Your Business*, and she speaks and conducts workshops and seminars for business associations on marketing and social media topics. She has conducted seminars for groups such as the Small Business Development Centers of Cecil and Harford County Maryland, Chambers of Commerce in Maryland and Delaware, the Midatlantic Direct Marketing Conference, the Small Business Survival Summit in Baltimore, and the University of Maryland Extension.

Connect with Apryl:

Website: http://aparcher.com
Facebook: www.facebook.com/aparchercopywriting
Twitter: www.twitter.com/apryl_parcher (@apryl_parcher)
Linkedin: www.Linkedin.com/in/aprylparchercopywriting
Google + : http://plus.ly/aprylparcher
Youtube: http://www.youtube.com/aprylparcher

Lou Bortone

Lou Bortone is an Online Branding Expert and Video Marketing Strategist who helps entrepreneurs and small business owners build breakthrough brands on the Internet so they can have more visibility, credibility and profitability. Lou delivers innovative and creative online branding strategies, including video marketing, social media marketing and online video coaching/consulting.

Lou has over 25 years of experience as a marketing executive in the TV and entertainment industries. He has worked for *E! Entertainment Television* and was Senior VP of Marketing & Advertising for *Fox Family Worldwide*, a division of *Fox* in Los Angeles. He is also an author and ghostwriter of six business books, and is a Certified Guerrilla Marketing Coach and a Book Yourself Solid Certified Coach. Learn more at www.LouBortone.com

Chris Brogan

Chris Brogan is president of a media and education company. He consults and speaks professionally with Fortune 100 and 500 companies like PepsiCo, General Motors, Microsoft, and more, about the intersection of business, technology and media. He is a New York Times bestselling co-author of *Trust Agents*, and a featured monthly columnist at *Entrepreneur Magazine*. Chris's blog, [chrisbrogan.com], is in the Top 5 of the Advertising Age Power150. He has over 12 years experience in online community, social media, and related technologies.

Rich Brooks

Rich Brooks is founder and president of Flyte New Media, a web design and Internet marketing firm in Portland, Maine.

His monthly Flyte Log email newsletter and web marketing blog cover topics such as search engine optimization, blogging, social media, email marketing, and building websites that sell. He is currently an Expert Blogger at *FastCompany.com* and a regular contributor at *SocialMediaExaminer.com.*

Rich is a nationally recognized speaker on entrepreneurship, internet marketing and social media. He is the "tech guru" on the WCSH Channel 6 evening news show, *207*, and teaches web marketing and social media courses for entrepreneurs at the University of Southern Maine Center for Continuing Education.

Pam Brossman

After 25 years in the Corporate Communications industry and the birth of her son Hunter, Pam decided the corporate life was no longer for her and went in search of a lifestyle change.

Pam launched *SheExperts.com* and *SheConnect* to help women entrepreneurs learn how to use their expertise and the power of digital marketing, digital branding, digital products and digital communications to build a successful business that gives them complete ownership of their career and lifestyle choices.

Pam is a highly sought after international speaker on the topic of digital marketing and digital communications, specializing in digital products and online training. Pam believes success is all about having a "Millionaire Attitude" and lives with her husband, son and huge Groodle puppy overlooking the ocean in Sydney, Australia. Her favorite pastime is hanging at the beach with her family and entertaining with friends when not working at home or cruising around the world.

Janice Clark

Janice Clark is the owner of BizMSolutions, a full service virtual solutions provider and social strategy firm. Her team of experienced virtual assistants includes marketing VAs, copywriters, graphic designers, web designers, Public Relations professionals and more. Together they help businesses across the globe leverage their social media efforts in order to increase their social and financial net worth.

In 2010 BizMSolutions launched a special report entitled "Hiring Out social media Tasks: How to Get Help Without Losing Control." The strategies used to launch this report resulted in a 25% increase in revenue for her company. Janice continues to use the same systems she created for the BizMSolutions launch to help her own clients gain recognition and bottom line results using social media.

Hollis Gillespie

Hollis Gillespie is a humorist, syndicated columnist, NPR

Commentator and top-selling author. Her column can be found monthly on the back page of every issue of *Atlanta Magazine.*

Hollis has appeared on the cover of numerous publications including *Atlanta Magazine*, *Creative Loafing* and *Tampa's Weekly Planet.* She has been profiled in *Marie Claire*, *Bust*, *Writer's Digest* and *Entertainment Weekly.*

Her television appearances include *The Tonight Show with Jay Leno*, *TBS Storyline*, *Monica Kaufman's Closeups*, *Good Day Atlanta*, and an upcoming appearance on *TV Land.* Her radio commentaries appear regularly on National Public Radio (NPR) and Georgia Public Broadcasting.

The film rights to her first book, *Bleachy-Haired Honky Bitch: Tales from a Bad Neighborhood*, are currently under option with a major Hollywood studio.

Elaine Lindsay

Elaine Lindsay is a partner in TROOL Social Media, a digital marketing firm with a concentration in social media and relationship marketing. TROOL Social Media's committed team employs a full menu of digital resources to help small to medium-sized business build their presence online and raise their bottom lines.

As an early adopter, Elaine attended the first-ever Google+ #NYC HIRL (Hangout in Real Life) and specializes in Google+. Her clients call her "The Social Media Maven."

Elaine is passionate about social media strategies and integration with SEO, and she tailors her clients' social media efforts to yield the most exposure and optimization through engagement.

Elaine's more than 25 years business experience include retail, accounting, web design, print media and business start-up consulting. This gives her a unique perspective in better understanding her clients' needs.

Paul Mosenson

For more than 20 years, Paul Mosenson has been building strategic, comprehensive multimedia marketing campaigns that get results. He possesses a unique expertise in traditional and interactive advertising and social media, and over the last few years has become a national thought leader on lead generation and content marketing. Paul's vast and versatile marketing experience spans the fields of healthcare, financial services, business-to-business, economic development, technology, retail, state-funded programs, automotive and tourism.

NuSpark Marketing is the firm Paul founded in early 2010 that offers clients a "lead management" approach. Paul utilizes a team of freelancers (design, content, social media and SEO) to support his vision and encompass the entire "lead-to-sale" process. Other marketing companies focus on specific elements, such as SEO, website design, copywriting, or conversion. However, NuSpark manages the entire process. Recently, Paul was named one of the top 50 lead generators in America by the Sales Lead Management Association. His blog is nationally recognized, and he's a writer of many successful e-books on lead generation and social media.

Amy Porterfield

Amy Porterfield is the co-author of *Facebook Marketing All-In-One for Dummies* and a Social Media Strategist. She creates educational programs for small businesses and entrepreneurs to help them get more traffic, leads and sales with social media marketing.

Amy's been in the marketing arena for over 12 years and spent over six years working alongside Peak Performance Coach,

Anthony Robbins, where she managed his content marketing team and major online marketing campaigns. Amy's most recent online program, *FB Influence*, teaches businesses and entrepreneurs how to grow a lucrative fan base, increase engagement and turn fans into buyers. Learn more at www.AmyPorterfield.com.

Ted Rubin

Ted is a leading social marketing strategist and in 2009 started using the term ROR: Return on Relationship™ — a concept he believes is the cornerstone for building an engaged multi-million member database, many of whom are vocal advocates for the brand, like the one he built for e.l.f. Cosmetics as the Chief Marketing Officer between 2008 and 2010, and the one being built for the new updated OpenSky where Ted was Chief Social Marketing Officer until the end of April 2011.

In May 2011, Ted announced leaving OpenSky and accepting the position of Chief Social Marketing Officer at Collective Bias (whose Advisory Board he joined in January 2011).

Ted is the most followed CMO on Twitter and has one of the deepest networks of any marketer in the social arena. ROR is the basis of his philosophy...It's All About Relationships!

Laura Rubinstein

Laura Rubinstein is a Certified Hypnotherapist, Author, and Social Media and Relationship Marketing Strategist for passionate business owners, celebrities, speakers and authors.

She is the President and co-founder of the Social Buzz Club and creator of the *Social Media Blast Off* course. Coach Laura helps her clients create a brand, buzz, and profitable and fulfilling relationships. With her 22-plus years of marketing experience and focus on relationship building, Laura has optimized marketing plans and developed branding strategies for more than a thousand business owners across the United States, the United Kingdom, Australia, and Canada.

Coach Laura regularly delivers keynotes, workshops, webinars and in-depth social media and relationship based marketing courses. Learn more and receive cutting edge social media tips from Laura at LauraOnSocialMedia.com and TransformToday.com.

Neal Schaffer

Neal Schaffer is a recognized leader in helping businesses and professionals embrace and strategically leverage the potential of social media. An author, speaker and social media strategy consultant, Neal has appeared in the *Wall Street Journal, Bloomberg Businessweek, Yahoo!*, and the *American Express Open Forum.*

A graduate of Amherst College, he is also fluent in Mandarin Chinese and Japanese and currently resides in Irvine, California, where he proudly serves on the marketing committee for the United Way of Orange County. Neal is the author of *Maximizing LinkedIn for Sales and social media Marketing* and founder of Windmill Networking.

Jesse Stay

Jesse Stay is a speaker, author, blogger, and entrepreneur who writes and consults on the topics of social media and new media architecture, bridging the gap between "technical" and "social" for both marketers and developers. Jesse has written four books — his latest two, *Facebook Application Development For*

Dummies, and the recently released *Google+ For Dummies* show the breadth of knowledge Jesse has to offer. Jesse was also named one of 20 developers to follow on Twitter and one of 10 entrepreneurs to follow on Twitter by the top Tech blog *Mashable.com*

His unique technology background has enabled him to help others understand the new mesh of technology, marketing, PR, and customer service which social media has come to be, and how people can deeply integrate these technologies into their own environments. Jesse has consulted for top 10 Facebook applications, large corporations, social media applications with millions of users, and has helped many people become successful through their social media efforts to merge technology with marketing.

Chris Treadaway

Chris Treadaway is the founder and CEO of Notice Technologies, a provider of local, real-time advertising platforms for newspapers, television and technology companies. He is also managing director of Ultrastart, a social media consulting firm that has consulted for major companies such as Microsoft, Land rover, Wiley Publishing, and the City of Austin, Texas.

Chris has worked in the Internet marketing field for more than 15 years and has an MBA from the University of Texas at Austin and a BA from Louisiana State University. He blogs regularly about entrepreneurship and social media issues at http://treadaway.typepad.com and on Twitter at www.twitter.com/treada.

Viveka Von Rosen

Viveka von Rosen started using LinkedIn in 2006 when she saw a presentation on the opportunities of Business Networking with

LinkedIn. Having doubled her own business with face-to-face networking, she saw the immense potential of a business online networking site.

Viveka is known internationally as the "LinkedIn Expert" and speaks to business owners, corporations, legal firms and associations on the benefits of marketing with social media, and in particular LinkedIn.

Currently writing *LinkedIn Marketing: An Hour A Day* for John Wiley & Sons, she is also a regular source on LinkedIn for prestigious news outlets such as *Mashable.com*, *SocialMediaExaminer.com* and *The Miami Herald.* She is the host of the biggest LinkedIn chat on Twitter: #LinkedInChat (Recently quoted by Mashable as one of the top 10 business blogs) and co-moderator of LinkedStrategies, the largest LinkedIn strategy group on LinkedIn. She is constantly learning, sharing and transferring social media skills and strategies to her tribe.

Denise Wakeman

Denise Wakeman is an Online Visibility Expert and Founder of The Blog Squad. She works with entrepreneurs and business professionals to leverage blogs and social media tools to boost their online visibility to get more traffic, leads, customers and opportunities.

Denise writes on two marketing blogs, is a co-author of best-selling books *Success Secrets of social media Superstars* and *Trust Your Heart: Transform Your Ideas into Income.* She frequently speaks at conferences about business blogging and how to gain expert status through social marketing. She has been quoted in *The Wall Street Journal*, *The Huffington Post*, *Newsday*, *Canada's National Post*, *FastCompany Online*, as well as many other online and offline publications. Denise was recently featured in the documentary film, *Women in Business 2.0.*

Blogging Tools

Twitterfeed: http://twitterfeed.com

Editorial Calendars

Kathryn & Apryl's Blog & Social Media Content Calendar: http://www.solvingthesocialmediapuzzle.com/calendar/.

Contest Applications

ContestBurner: http://www.contestburner.com
EasyPromo: http://www.easypromosapp.com
North Social: http://northsocial.com
Strutta: http://www.strutta.com
Wildfire App: http://www.wildfireapp.com

Customer Service Software

Parature: http://www.parature.com/

Email Applications

Constant Contact: http://www.constantcontact.com/index.jsp
Emailvision: http://emailvision.com
LinkedIn Inmail: http://www.dummies.com/how-to/content/how-to-send-a-linkedin-inmail0.html
MailChimp: http://mailchimp.com/

Facebook Developers

Lujure: http://lujure.com
Tabsite:http://www.tabsite.com

Online Meeting Applications

AnyMeeting: http://www.anymeeting.com
GoToMeeting: http://www.gotomeeting.com
MeetingBurner: http://www.meetingburner.com

RSS Feed Readers

Google Reader: www.google.com/reader

Small Business Success Examples

Michael Sinkin, DDS: http://michaelsinkindds.com/
Hyper Martial Arts: http://hypermartialarts.com/
VoIP Supply: http://www.voipsupply.com/

Search Tools:

Google Trends: http://www.google.com/trends
Twitter Search: http://search.twitter.com

Social Content Schedulers/Aggregators

Buffer: http://bufferapp.com
Hootsuite: http://hootsuite.com
SocialOomph: http://www.socialoomph.com
TweetDeck: http://www.tweetdeck.com
paper.li: http://paper.li

Social Media Marketing Applications

Awareness Social Marketing Hub: http://www.awarenessnetworks.com/why-the-hub
Spredfast: http://spredfast.com/about/

Social Media Measurement/Monitoring Tools

Crowdbooster: http://crowdbooster.com
Facebook Insights: http://www.facebook.com/help/?faq=268680253165747#How-do-I-access-Page-Insights?
Profile Stats Pro (for LinkedIn): http://learn.linkedin.com/the-homepage/profilestats/
LinkedIn Signal: http://blog.linkedin.com/2010/09/29/linkedin-signal/
Radian6: http://www.radian6.com
Raven Tools: http://raventools.com/internet-marketing-tools/social-media-monitor/
Scout Labs: http://lithium.com/
Sprout Social: http://sproutsocial.com/features/social-media-monitoring
Social Report: http://www.socialreport.com/
Twitalyzer: http://twitalyzer.com/
Woopra: http://www.woopra.com/
YouTube Analytics: http://support.google.com/youtube/bin/answer.py?hl=en&answer=1270714

Social Sharing Websites

The Social Buzz Club: http://www.socialbuzzclub.com Triberr: http://triberr.com

Surveys

Survey Monkey: http://www.surveymonkey.com

Twitter Tools

Tweet Chat: http://tweetchat.com
Twellow: http://www.twellow.com
Wefollow: http://wefollow.com

Website Analytics

Clicky: http://getclicky.com/
Google Analytics: www.google.com/analytics/

WordPress Plugins

Digg Digg: http://wordpress.org/extend/plugins/digg-digg/
TwitterTools: http://wordpress.org/extend/plugins/twitter-tools/
Sexy Bookmarks:
http://wordpress.org/extend/plugins/sexy-bookmarks-sidebar-plugin/

Writing Services

Textbroker: http://www.textbroker.com
Endnotes

Endnotes

1 TheSocialSkinny.com, (2012), 100 More Social Media Statistics for 2012, http://thesocialskinny.com/100-more-social-media-statistics-for-2012/

2 NeilsenWire. (2009). Global Advertising: Consumers Trust Real Friends and Virtual Strangers the Most, http://blog.nielsen.com/ nielsenwire/consumer/global-advertising-consumers-trust-real-friends-and-virtual-strangers-the-most/

3 OnlineMBA. (2012). Infographic: A Case Study in Social Media Demographics, http://www.onlinemba.com/blog/social-media-demographics/

4 Allfacebook.com. (2012). Uh Oh, Facebook Pages Only Reach 17% of Fans, http://allfacebook.com/facebook-page-17_b73948

5 Mashable.com (2011). Infographic: Why Do People Follow Brands? http://mashable.com/2011/06/30/why-people-follow-brands/

6 DDB. (2011). Facebook Study Results: The Evolution of Facebook Fans, http://www.ddb.com/ddblogs/strategy/ddb-paris-in-collaboration-wit.html

7 Allfacebook.com. (2011). The 7 Biggest Fan Page Marketing Mistakes, http://allfacebook.com/7-biggest-fan-page-marketing-mistakes_b43011

8 Visibli A Study of Fan Engagement on Facebook Pages April 19, 2011 http://visibli.com/reports/fbstudy

9 Kissmetrics.com, (2011). The Science of Social Timing Part 1: Social Networks, http://blog.kissmetrics.com/science-of-social-timing-1/

10 Digital Surgeons Facebook vs. Twitter Infographic http://www.digitalsurgeons.com/facebook-vs-twitter-infographic/

11 Harvard Business Review. (2009). Men Follow Men and Nobody Tweets, http://blogs.hbr.org/cs/2009/06/new_twitter_research_men _follo.html

12 YouTube statistics: http://www.youtube.com/t/press_statistics

13 CSNBC. (2011). NetNet: Kenneth Cole Puts Well-Heeled Foot in Mouth, http://www.cnbc.com/id/41410463/Kenneth_Cole_Puts _Well_Heeled_Foot_in_Mouth

14 CBSNEWS. (2012) Techtalk: KFC Tailand apologizes for improper Facebook quake posting, http://www.cbsnews.com/8301-501465_162-57413187-501465/kfc-thailand-apologizes-for-improper-facebook-quake-posting/

15 Ragan's PR Daily, (2011). 5 Social Media Blunders and How to Avoid Them, http://www.prdaily.com/Main/Articles/5_social_media _blunders_and_how_to_avoid_them_8360.aspx

16 ViralBlog. (2009). Why Ryanair Needs a Social Marketing Agency, http://www.viralblog.com/social-media/why-ryanair-needs-a-social-marketing-agency/

CPSIA information can be obtained
at www.ICGtesting.com
Printed in the USA
LVOW04s2010211016
509751LV00008B/840/P